theatre & law

Alan Read

macmillan education · palgrave

First published 2016 by
PALGRAVE

Palgrave in the UK is an imprint of Macmillan Publishers Limited, registered in England, company number 785998, of 4 Crinan Street, London, N1 9XW.

Palgrave Macmillan in the US is a division of St Martin's Press LLC, 175 Fifth Avenue, New York, NY 10010.

Palgrave is a global imprint of the above companies and is represented throughout the world.

Palgrave® and Macmillan® are registered trademarks in the United States, the United Kingdom, Europe and other countries.

ISBN 978–1–137–46955–7

This book is printed on paper suitable for recycling and made from fully managed and sustained forest sources. Logging, pulping and manufacturing processes are expected to conform to the environmental regulations of the country of origin.

A catalogue record for this book is available from the British Library.

A catalog record for this book is available from the Library of Congress.

Printed in China

theatre & law

Theatre &
Series Editors: Jen Harvie and Dan Rebellato

Published

Forthcoming

Theatre&
Series Standing Order ISBN 978–0–230–20327–3

You can receive future titles in this series as they are published by placing a standing order. Please contact your bookseller or, in case of difficulty, write to us at the address below with your name and address, the title of the series and the ISBN quoted above.

Customer Services Department, Macmillan Distribution Ltd, Houndmills, Basingstoke, Hampshire, RG21 6XS, UK

part one: within the law: ten rules of engagement

There are courtrooms, judges and lawyers. And then there is, or there *was,* as it often came first, the performance, or the memory of the actor's performance, of that judge or lawyer. Sometimes our perceptions of the chronological relations between law and performance mislead us along these fault lines of recall. Harper Lee's 'courtroom classic', *To Kill a Mockingbird* (1960) is perhaps better known *as* a courtroom classic because of the performance of Gregory Peck as the idealistic lawyer Atticus Finch in the film version of the book (1962). In the novel the trial of Tom Robinson takes barely a few pages, but it is the drama of the court that prevails in recollection. *Twelve Angry Men*, initially a TV play broadcast in the early 1950s, then a stage play, then a film directed by Sidney Lumet in 1957, is recalled by many people of a certain age as they take up jury service in the shadow of Henry Fonda's 'juryman'. For some, Arthur Miller's classic dramatic work *The Crucible* (1953) plays out parallels between the Salem witch trials and the McCarthy Communist purges of the US in the 1950s. For Norman Mailer it was 'just a play about a bad marriage' (Doughty, 2014).

I would guess that if you have picked up this book, you are less a Mailerite and more predisposed to thinking there is something 'at stake' when one speaks about the relations between theatre and law. Having just referred to *The Crucible*, it should not go without saying that as well as something 'being at stake' in the relations between theatre and law, *someone* might also be 'at stake', literally. The simple fact that such summary 'justice' is widespread in the form of genocides should alert us to our responsibility precisely to establish as rationally as we can where legal processes benefit from their relations with the public, the performative and the spectacular, and where they are complicated and sometimes diminished by their continuous relationship with theatricality. With respect to law, Jaques was not quite right when he said in Shakespeare's *As You Like It*: 'All the world's a stage' (Act II, Scene VII). There may well be affects that I experience, feelings that are responsive to theatrical things in the world. But there are certainly *effects* that decisively distance some acts from others, and not least of all in the realm of legal action. These effects, outcomes and judgments which constrain or secure liberties remind me that any 'theatre real', with its portrayal of such incarcerations and freedoms, is to be carefully distinguished from that worldly 'real real', if only for the sake of just action in and on that very world.

There are some obvious ways in which theatre and law are related, and there are some less obvious ways in which the operations of one depend upon the conduct of the other for what each can do. In the following pages I will explore these sometimes obvious and sometimes obscure relations. I will provide by way of opening a 'simple to use' guide to ten principles of performance within law to establish how law is, if it is anything, a performative mode of practice. In the second part of the book, I will examine a judgment in law and through that judgment ascertain how law is inscribed within everyday practices that effect a considerable proportion of my potential readership. I will offer a close reading of a canonical theatrical work from the perspective of law and anthropology and build that reading outwards from my own subject position, which is, I will argue, always contained within legal precedents. I will undertake an analysis of an internationally celebrated theatre production where law, performance and politics are codependent and witnessed in practice, and to conclude I will consider ways in which humans are 'de-personed' by law, and how artists have rendered such matters within their recent work. The book will end with some further reading in each of these, and other, areas where law and theatre relate.

So, let's begin by returning to my first example in a more contemporary setting. Sometimes confusion between law and its performance does not need dramatically trained actors like Gregory Peck or Henry Fonda to complicate due process. To watch Johnnie Cochran, the defence lawyer for OJ Simpson, running rings around common sense in the Superior Court of Los Angeles in 1994, or Lt Col. Vermeulen demonstrating for Oscar Pistorius's defence lawyer, Barry Roux, to the Pretoria court in 2014 how a cricket bat was used to break down the bathroom door behind which Reeva Steenkamp lay dying, is to remind us that the relations between law and performance are already, without sanctioned 'actors', quite complicated enough by spectacle and rhetoric.

But while complicated, these divides and relations are not indecipherable. It is performance studies rather than jurisprudence, the word coined to articulate the philosophy of the law in the early 1600s, that has given us some helpful vocabulary to unravel these relations. For instance Gregory Peck and Henry Fonda are conducting what I would like to call 'meta-performances'. They relate to the performances of the second group (Cochran and Roux) by means of a secondary order of mimetic behaviours. This symbiotic relationship between the law and its image, legal process and its performance, reaches back from the 'Nordic Noir' legal series of today's television media, in series such as *The Killing* and *The Bridge*, 2500 years to the Greek agora of 5th century BCE Athens. It is a relationship presented in Aristophanes' *The Wasps* (422 BCE), staged as part of the Lenaia festival, in which a son attempts to cure his court-obsessed father, a 'trialophile', with a staging of a court case between two household dogs. And it is a relationship presented in *Arguendo* by Elevator Repair Service (2013) at New York's Public Theatre, in which a verbatim version of a 1991 Supreme Court case, *Barnes v Glen Theatre*, involving the right to 'dance nude', is played out. And, I would propose, it is these acts that also rhetorically fashion and frame our experiences of what stands for legal behaviours in the first place. To say that law has been ubiquitous to the repertoire of theatre since its inception might be obvious, but if so, it is well worth considering why.

The first group of practitioners I have just been discussing, you could call them 'actor lawyers', including those in *The Wasps* and *Arguendo*, 'perform-perform' their roles; the second group, 'lawyers', you could say, simply (if legal process could ever be simple) 'perform' those roles. Simple or not, they *are* performing those roles and are symbolically invested as such, as lawyers, to do so. What we often recall when we say the word 'law' in English, first used at the time of Ethelred in around 1000, is somebody performing (whom I might call an actor), 'somebody who is performing legal process' (whom I could call a lawyer). It is this *secondary* rendition of the act of the prosecution or defence that has become the common model for our understanding of the law. And this is for the obvious reason that statistically speaking most people have never set foot in a courtroom or been involved in a criminal inquiry, yet the majority of those with access to electricity and a TV signal have witnessed such things over and over again.

When I walk with my students the short distance over the Strand in central London from their university to the Royal Courts of Justice to witness an appeal hearing from the well of the courtroom, very few of them have ever been inside this building despite the fact there is a prominent and surprisingly welcoming sign outside: OPEN TO THE PUBLIC. Why is the second highest court in the land open to the public? That is perhaps one of the key reference points of this book, and the publication of this book in 2015 marks an anniversary that shapes everything it is about. For it is the necessary *openness* of the law, at least in its Common Law version in the Anglo-American tradition, that distinguishes its practice over 800 years, since the signing of the Magna Carta of 1215.

I will concentrate in this book on Common Law (as distinct to the codified structure of Civil Law or Islamic 'Sharia' Law), not because it is without robust critique; quite the contrary, as since Hobbes' *Leviathan* (1651), Common Law has been almost continuously under scrutiny for its often unspoken affirmation of a seamless continuity between past and present, for its customary and unwritten form and for its apparently 'immemorial nature'. The international reach of Common Law systems has always been cognizant, through successive moderations, from Hobbes' *Dialogue* (1681, 1971), via Jeremy Bentham's *Introduction to Principles of Morals and Legislation* (1789), to John Austin's *The Province of Jurisprudence Determined* (1832), of the rhetorical flair upon which its operations depended. Successive commentators sustained the idea, if not the reality, that the proliferation of Common Law and its perceived success was predicated on its unique ability to present innovation as the 'continuity of tradition'. Indeed, even Ronald Dworkin's relatively recent *Law's Empire* (1986) perpetuated this principle of perceived 'continuity' over the temporary reversals of 'case-based law' central to the Civil Law tradition, as Philippe Raynaud has made clear (Cassin, 2014, pp. 550–558).

My deployment of Common Law as the legal ground of this book does profit from these rhetorical traditions and their inherent theatricality, but it really has more to do with the potential readership of *Theatre & Law* and the book's reach amongst, primarily, English-speaking readers. Without for a moment having to endorse Fernanda Pirie's Anglo-centric view in *The Anthropology of Law* that law is 'a category of the English-speaking world' (2013, pp. 4–5), it *is* Common Law systems that for good or ill (and the British Empire is as much to blame for this as anything) preside over and through a third of the world's populations, 2.5 billion people and counting. So what I am discussing in this book may not be a human universal, indeed its adherents number less than those circumscribed by Civil Law, but it *does* have historically related links to the peoples of India, Pakistan, Nigeria, Ghana, Bangladesh, the United Kingdom, South Africa, New Zealand, Ireland, North America, Israel and Australia, amongst many others. To give a concrete example of how such 'openness' – an openness, I suggest, secured through the means of performances of various kinds – was embedded in the development of Common Law in particular, one might consider the centrality of the writ of *habeas corpus* in anglophone legal culture from the early 1600s. Simply put, as Paul Halliday lays out in his comprehensive history of the idea, *habeas corpus* describes the process, 'to bring a prisoner before a judge in order "to signify the

7

crimes laid against him" and thereby to ensure that law is honored in holding or releasing him' (2010, p. 2). *Habeas corpus* enshrined the principle in law that for a trial to take place the defendant had to be 'made to appear', a theatrical manifestation if ever there was one. Accused persons had to be *present* in order to be able to defend themselves.

The words '*habeas corpus*' do not appear as such in the Magna Carta. That concept was to develop from the 17th century onwards, but its origins appear in the many 'liberties' awarded by the Magna Carta, including number 39 of the 63 that made up the charter that reads: 'No free man shall be arrested or imprisoned ... except by the lawful judgment of his peers or by the law of the land' (2010, p. 15). This 'openness', partly represented through *habeas corpus* but also through other processes of publicity, is critical to the conduct of law because despite the fact very few of us statistically will ever conduct ourselves in relation to the legal process, we are all, as the French philosopher and historian of ideas Michel Foucault pointed out, circumscribed by the law (*Discipline and Punish*, 1975). It is not that we *will* require the services of the courts in our lives, as we almost certainly will not, it is that we *might*. And this 'might' requires us to be cognizant of what the law could do for us, or to us. It might discipline or punish us. It will certainly determine us, as my consideration of the anthropology of law will lay out in the second part of this book.

As my first rule of engagement between performance and law I will suggest that law has to be *seen* to be done. It is not adequate nor indeed technically 'legal' in Common Law cultures for a legal system to do its work in private (though the continued scandal of Camp X Ray at Guantanamo Bay at the time of writing immediately introduces a note of caution to any such claim). Yes, cases can be declared in the Common Law system as 'in camera' (literally 'in a chamber', from the Latin root), but otherwise the law must show itself, must reveal itself in action. In so doing, it is of course *showing doing*, one of the prerequisites that the performance theorist Richard Schechner demands for something to be called performance in the first place (*Essays on Performance Theory*, 1976). Performances are precisely constituted through a conscious act of 'showing doing' involving some form of agent and some form of audience.

Secondly, law presents a workable narrative for drama as it commonly involves a beginning, a middle and an end. While Charles Dickens in his novel *Bleak House* (1852/2003) and Franz Kafka in his parable *Before the Law* (1915/2005) emphasize the longevity of the law, its intractability, the vast majority of cases that are brought to trial come to judgment. For law to function, decisions have to be made. This should not go without saying. While practices I will consider under the rubric of theatre in this book range from the conventional Brechtian structure of *The Caucasian Chalk Circle* to the less conformist performance practices of the Palestinian theatre company ShiberHur, each of these forms seems to have drawn at least some of its specifically theatrical energy, as we shall see, from the structure offered it by the urgency of legal narratives.

9

The 'drama' of probate, the 'reading of the will', and its pictorial representation in 19th-century English painting traditions, provides just such a history of narrative urgency, with its overriding dynamics of 'beginning', the gathering of the family, 'middle', the reading of the will, and 'end', the fallout from the declaration. As Daniel Monk suggests, the will is the most represented of legal texts amongst legal documents, despite the simple fact that wills were, and are, very rarely 'read' in such an obviously dramatic way. In the 19th century the place of probate in literature reached its height with readings of wills amongst assembled families and claimants commonplace in the work of Charles Dickens, Anthony Trollope, Emile Zola and Walter Scott. George Elliot's *Middlemarch* (1874) features no less than three wills which braid with the shifting concerns of capital and property explored in that work. But these readings disappear as quickly as they appeared, by the 20th century almost completely. By the time Joan Crawford's will was read to her family in May 1977, including the notorious tenth codicil, 'It is my intention to make no provision herein for my son Christopher or my daughter Christina for reasons which are well known to them' (Chandler, 2008), the prominence of the dramatic reading had all but gone from film and theatrical representation.

This rather literal narrative symmetry between the dramatic urgency of legal processes such as these and performance should immediately be complicated by a third idea proposed by Aoife Monks in response to a speaker at the *Performing the Law* conference that took place at the French

Institute in London in 2014. There Monks asked whether perhaps the law acted as a form of *surrogate*, and in so doing she wondered whether the point of representations of the law might be a means through which audiences reach for something else. I am attracted to this idea as I do not for a moment think that watching plays about legal matters, such as *The Colour of Justice* (1999), concerning the Stephen Lawrence Inquiry, in which the appalling narrative of a racist murder on the streets of London in 1993 was replayed from court testimonies, work *as theatre* because they are about legal matters per se. I think they work theatrically because they are about human animals in a very precise form of representational crisis which connects this experience, the one in the theatre, with others elsewhere we have had or wish to imagine, where power and its contestation are at stake. In the case of *The Colour of Justice* it was the entire criminal justice system that was really on trial for its institutional failure to pursue even the rudiments of justice for the victim's family.

A fourth association between theatre and law might be drawn from Victor Turner, the Catholic anthropologist, who reminds us quite simply that performance needs *experience* to do what it does (*From Ritual to Theatre*, 1982). The most obvious level of association between performance and law might be the rendering of such experience in the form of storytelling. For Turner the 'rendering of experience' requires us to 'try something', to test something out, and it is in such playing that we give ourselves the opportunity to understand experience, and in a sense, to 'experience experience'.

Turner's concept of 'working through' would appear to be shared by performance and the law, allowing people to work through something they have just become aware of. And, importantly, both performance and law allow us to *process* that thing we call experience. Not all practices mobilize or facilitate the processing of experience. Indeed some seem precisely to have been invented and sponsored by governments and multinational corporations because of their bromide-like, perennial anti-processural quality. Think of mass spectator sports, and especially football, which in the UK at least in its annual cycle of predictable moneyed outcomes operates to efface its cyclical nature. The quarter-century scandal that denied justice to the families of Liverpool football supporters suffocated at the Hillsborough Stadium on 15 April 1989, one of the world's worst football disasters, would be one measure of where the most extreme experience could not (was not allowed to) be 'processed' with any fidelity to the truth. The sober truth was that up until this time football supporters were treated to all intents and purposes as nascent criminals by the authorities responsible for their care.

A fifth association between theatre and the law is the means by which a judicial spectacle operates simultaneously as a 'reality' and a 'fiction'. For a spectacular event to occur, 'something has to happen'. We have established above that the law is a place where something certainly happens. It operates through *action*, not just a mental operation. It is made up of performing and spectating. It occurs in a specific time and place. And it is defined by the intersubjectivity of its participants. In other words, both parties have to agree to the status of the event for it to be viable and function. So, as Guy Spielmann proposed at the *Performing the Law* conference at the French Institute referred to earlier, in each of these senses at least, a court trial meets all the criteria one might wish for in a spectacular event. As Spielmann is quick to point out though, all this is very well but has little to do with justice, which after all one would have thought was the *raison d'être* of the law. We have the law 'as it should function' in the interests of justice, and we have the 'law as it does function'. And importantly we have a critical valence of the law, which relates to this book especially, and provides us with the sixth point of contact between theatre and law, that is we have the law as it is *perceived* to function. The phrase 'justice has been served' suggests that such justice was once breached but has now been remedied, but such easy pieties obscure a complex of problematic performances.

Justice at all times remains to be defined and enforced; it is not *only* an ontological aspect of the natural world, despite what I will argue in the second section of this book in defining the legal identity of the human, '*Homo Juridicus*'. You could say it requires something the legal writer Gary Watt names with a neologism, 'Per*force*mance', to establish itself, a force that Walter Benjamin, Michel Foucault and Louis Althusser all subscribe to in their writing. Just think of the variety of means of 'summary justice' that you have come across to put into question such a condition of natural or inevitable justice. A Kangaroo Court, a 'mock court' in every sense of that phrase, would be an obvious example. Or think of the laws that 'we' all believe do not serve justice, such as the widespread homophobic laws of the 20th century or racist laws that persist into the 21st. Or, concomitantly, the number of times that we hear of 'justice' being served, or at least someone else's idea of justice, without any recourse to law courts, or legal processes, of any kind. Many of us might not be attracted to Charles Bronson's gun-toting character in the 1974 film *Death Wish*, or Judge Dredd's mantra 'I am the Law', but there are some who are, and we ignore these forms of 'justice' at our peril.

If I think theatre, performance and especially live art have privileged the special and defining characteristic of present-ness, the 'ontology' of its liveness over the last four decades, then for my seventh reflection on theatre and law I would like to recall that the performance field has nothing on the legal system when it comes to foregrounding the palpable, and necessarily 'open', present of its workings. Here the importance, indeed the fetishization of public-ness of law, has at least equalled that of the theatrical domain, and here the value of 'liveness' at all costs is upheld to the extent that one might think of the law itself as the privileged site of the 'live' in the 21st century. The long-running debate about televising court proceedings (as has long been the case in the US) has returned the UK judicial system to an argument over intricacies of 'liveness' that Peggy Phelan and Philip Auslander prepared us for in their disagreements over the relations between the live and the mediatized in performance in the 1990s.

When I talk of experience 'working something through' I would want also to recognize in my eighth association the *time* of this working through in law, and what such duration introduces to the process by way of opportunity and entropy. The avalanche of procedural papers that opens Charles Dickens's novel *Bleak House* figures this cumulative threat to justice as one bound by glacial time. Here the rhythm of the effective (the really happening) of the legal process, in all its real-time frailty, and the virtual version of that effective practice (the performance) in all its brushed-up and brushed-out niceties, become starkly contrasted. If I say at the conclusion of a *performance*, 'You are free to go', it is meaningless in anything but theatrical effect. Because I have no authority to say this, but also because no 'serious' time, or rather not the right 'real' time, has been spent on providing the conditions for such a statement, despite the theatrical time it has passed. If a judge says it, then 'you go free', but only after an acknowledged *time* of appropriate conduct has been committed to it. But why exactly is this?

We have J. L. Austin to thank for a primer, a taxonomy of these kinds of utterance that distinguish certain uses of language from what are called 'propositional utterances', mere statements of fact. He is interested in examples in which to say something is to 'do' something, and he outlined these conditions of utterance in a lecture series written up and published as *How to Do Things With Words* (1962). Here he described three valences where to say something is to do something. I am particularly interested in the third of these to explain the conundrum posed above,

15

but the first two need distinguishing. To 'say something' is of course to 'do something' at the basic level of sonic production, to perform a locutionary act through noise-making that corresponds to an accepted and understood vocabulary and grammar. Secondly, to say something on occasions is to perform an illocutionary act, it is a 'performative' in the sense that a phrase like 'I object' performs one's intentions in a court of law or a debate. But most interestingly there are also, thirdly, phrases, when used in certain circumstances, that carry a particular ritual and social force that effects a *further action*, beyond the thing being uttered. The officiating court clerk announcing the phrase 'The court is sitting' does not just mean the legal process is underway, it corroborates the validity of those decisions made therein. An utterance that passes judgment is also just such a phrase of doing as much as saying. 'You are guilty of murder' will, if spoken in an agreed and legitimate context of law-making and procedure, in all but the most anarchic of circumstances, mobilize secondary effects of incarceration or even execution.

Notoriously and problematically (for theatre specialists at least), Austin precisely excluded the contexts of theatre and staged performance from those in which such performatives could operate felicitously. But John Searle in his follow up work *Speech Acts: An Essay in the Philosophy of Language* (1969) further formalizes these 'felicitous' conditions of utterances while foregrounding the successful communication of the speaker's intention against a complex and contingent background. In this context speech directly precipitates action on the story level (such as through promises, threats or wooing), whether in courtrooms *or* dramatic dialogue. This finessing of the relations between what I would like to call the 'effective' and the 'virtual' domains of the relations between the primary performance of law, and its secondary rendering through theatre, is thus here further complicated, and this idea is something I will return to when I discuss the fascinating, legally inspired installation artwork of Carey Young.

While the discussions of performatives has over the last four decades rambled, often unhelpfully, far and wide from Austin and Searle's forensic clarity in their foundational work, there is one specific modality of the performative that demands attention in a book considering the relations between theatre and law, and it provides the ninth relation between their operations. That is the oath – a statement that often begins something like, 'I swear by …' and describes a solemn vow. An oath does not concern a statement, as such, but is the guarantee of the statement's efficacy, within a court and other contexts. An oath 'guarantees' the truth and efficacy of language, and for centuries in the courtroom setting an oath has been accompanied by the presentation of the hand to the courtroom to demonstrate that the hand remains unmarked (a throwback perhaps to a time when instances of previous criminality would be etched or tattooed on the palm of the offender). This overtly theatrical act, the combination of a gesture with a phrase, purports to secure the words used in some form of truth event, or as Émile Benveniste puts it, an 'oral rite': 'Its function consists not in the affirmation that it produces, but in the relation that it institutes between the word pronounced and the potency invoked' (Agamben, 2011, p. 4).

Giorgio Agamben's take on the significance of the oath is one predicated on a crisis *for* the oath. Paolo Prodi's work *Il sacramento del potere* (*The Sacrament of Power*, 1992) provided a comprehensive historical archaeology of the oath and came to the conclusion that while central to the specificity and vitality of Western Christian culture, its recent decline corresponds to a 'crisis in which the very being of man as a political animal is at stake' (2011, p. 1). Indeed, in a 2001 review of the UK court system, Lord Justice Auld recommended reforms of the declaration process, acknowledging that 'a combination of archaic words invoking God as the guarantor of proposed evidence and the perfunctory manner in which they are usually uttered detracts from, rather than underlines, the solemnity of the undertaking' (O'Brien, 2012). As the first generation to live beyond the centrality of the oath as a 'solemn and total, sacredly anchored bond to a political body', and rather in a world of secularized 'affirmation' of our willingness to speak with honesty, Agamben would contest that we now find ourselves on the threshold of a 'new form of political association' (2011, p. 1). That shift starts with the loosening of a previous bond between the living being and its language, with a consequence that Agamben summarizes in characteristically apocalyptic terms: 'When the ethical – and not simply cognitive – connection that unites words, things and human actions is broken, this in fact promotes a spectacular and unprecedented proliferation of vain words on the one hand and, on the other, of legislative apparatuses that seek obstinately to legislate on every aspect of that life on which they seem no longer to have any hold' (2011, p. 71). I will come to the socially deleterious consequences of such proliferation in the final section of this book.

The tenth and last of my associations between theatre and law is perhaps the most obvious and yet most misunderstood: the capacity for lawyers and judges to costume and bewig themselves. This is where most reflections upon the relations between theatre and law commonly begin and end, and that is not necessarily a bad thing. Judicial robes date back to the toga, and, as such, from its earliest incarnation the robe begins to allow for the separation of the professional from the nonlawyer, of course carrying with it the remnant of a certain priest-like quality of ministration.

But when pointing out the absurdity of the UK barrister's deployment of the wig, now perched in a reduced form on the top of their head like some comical hairy hat, is to forget that the lawyer is never, indeed *was* never (according to Gary Watt), meant to feel comfortable in the second skin of their legal office. They should find the robes of office irritating, ensuring they are alive to the formality and culture of the law as distinct to the nature of the community from which their appellants come. After all, the lawyer stands at the threshold of an individual's life, their freedom or their loss of liberty. Indeed, in the UK legal system judges and barristers have to be robed and bewigged when the case might determine the defendant's right to liberty.

The complexity of reading such costumed signs is well demonstrated by Michel Pastoureau in his work *The Devil's Cloth: A History of Stripes and Striped Fabric* (1991). In his essay therein on 'The Order and Disorder of the Stripe', he catalogues the historical shifts that stripes on cloth and clothing represented: 'the contemporary period has very much made itself the receptacle of all these practices and all the earlier codes, since coexisting within it are stripes that remain diabolic (those by which prisoners in death camps were ignominiously marked) or dangerous (those used for traffic signs and signals, for example) and others, that over time, have become hygienic (those on sheets and under-wear), playful (those used for leisure and sports clothes), or emblematic (those on uniforms, insignia, and flags)' (p. 4). For male solicitors and barristers in the 19th- and 20th-century legal systems, the pinstripe, just so wide but not too wide for fear of falling over into the diabolic, was the costume of choice for court appearance; a uni-form, yes, but also an emblematic flag as wide as the girth of many who wore its vertical pronouncement of rectitude so snugly. Recognizing the gender bias of any such analy-sis is a helpful reminder of the gender split that prevailed in UK courtrooms well into the 21st century. In 2012 only 23% of high court judges in England and Wales were women, with only Azerbaijan and Armenia having a lower ratio (Bowcott, 2012). Simultaneously donning ubiquitous pinstripe acknowledges the peculiar way the otherwise 'showy' male advocate might wish to neutralize something of his behaviour through the choice of such a common cloth.

So costuming in law is perhaps the inversion of costuming within the theatre. While worn individually, and with flashes of idiosyncratic flair by extroverts such as Michael Mansfield, QC, in the court room costuming operates to *efface* the individuality of the legal operators while cumulatively establishing the one thing we must all recognize: the singular face of the law. The face the law makes, as Gary Watt puts it, is critical to the law's public persona. He tells the story that when Viscount Kilmur, one of the prosecutors at the Nuremberg Trials, in December 1955 wrote to Sir Ian Jacob, Military Assistant to Sir Winston Churchill, Viscount Kilmur summed up the commonly held presumption that this book would probably need to contest if it is to get very far: 'It is inappropriate for the law to be associated with anything that could be associated with entertainment.'

The face the law makes is one that clearly has to be on show, and seriously so, if Viscount Kilmur is to be taken at face value. The recent debates that Judge Peter Murphy presided over at Blackfriars Crown Court in London in 2013, concerning the rightness or not of permitting the Niqab to be worn in court proceedings in the UK, plays a particularly sensitive part in any such deliberation. On the one hand it would appear the height of cultural oppression to deny a woman the right to veil herself as she wishes. But it is the peculiar fascination of the law with its own faces, and the faces of the accused, that has fuelled this most recent of dilemmas that, after all, has as much a performative dimension as it does a legal one. But why *is* that, and why does performance lie at the heart of the Common Law system?

Well, these 'rules of engagement' I am laying out here between performance and law are by their nature only rules because they are written down. And in the deployment of the English language for this book, and especially so because we are talking about something called *Theatre & Law*, one set of things can be said and another set of things cannot be said. This is obvious when one looks at the breadth and diversity of the European tradition of legal concepts from Roman Law, systematically laid out in *The Dictionary of Untranslateables* (Cassin, 2014) with names such as *loi* and *droit* in French, *gesetx* and *recht* in German and *ley* and *derecho* in Spanish. I am barely equipped to deal with these linguistic varieties, never mind launch out into wholly distinct languages and modes as embodied within the great historic traditions of law in cultures such as the Yoruba dating from the 12th century or the 'Customary Law' of aboriginal peoples.

In English the word 'law' has a much wider extension as a concept than 'right' or its French equivalent *droit*, and it is wholly bound up with the millennia-long emergence of its codes and practices embedded in *institutions* with their own historical determinants (which themselves in each of these places have their own traditions of emergence). These are not just any institutions, but ones where the premium is on a certain kind of ceremonial as performance. It was the courts of the English Kingdom (within the context of a parliamentary system) from the Magna Carta in 1215 to the Bill of Rights in 1689 that according to Philippe Raynaud played a major role in the unification of English law, producing a law that was both 'customary' and based on 'case law', while providing the royal power with the centralized structure that was needed in order to govern (Cassin, 2014).

Now, for our purposes here it is important to emphasize that this Common Law was never meant to appear like a 'judge-made' law; it was, rather, conceived in the way it was to be *revealed*, performatively, by a judge who 'became' the mouthpiece for the law. This is a further reason why it is Common Law rather than the Statute Law (made by authorities) or Equity (the *rules* that supplement the Common Law), the other two pillars of the English justice system, that detain me in this book. If the first rule of law is 'precedent', which it is, then it is this conveyancing of the customary nature of its previous practices, through a form of restored behaviour as judicial ventriloquism, that becomes the performative frame of the Common Law system.

The rules of engagement between theatre and law that I have laid out above thus involve not only shared practices, each historically specific and mediated by cultural continuities, but also *principles*. On the one hand this book has begun to trace out where these practices coalesce and differ and the consequences of such association, and on the other, between these historically specific examples, I have explored the perhaps more pressing problem of how the very principles of law, as embedded within practices such as oath-taking, the presentation of the defendant for trial known as *habeas corpus* and the probate or will of the dead, are by their nature *already* principles of performance.

So, by way of conclusion to these 'rules of engagement', what if I were to propose, picking up on an idea proposed by Gary Watt, the rather outlandish idea that it is not that lawyers have always pretended to be stage actors (although it is quite obvious from the most cursory observation in the world's courtrooms that many of them do), but rather that stage actors have always pretended to be lawyers? What difference might such an inversion make to our understanding of the history of theatre itself?

The pervasiveness of the law and its rhetoric from a time well before the first actor, Thespis (534 BCE), was clearly evident to everyone, not just Plato and Aristotle. Plato's *Laws*, written in the form of dialogue, runs to a substantial 12 books, after all, and represents one of his longest works. Aristotle's *Poetics* by contrast, his template for dramatic theory and practice, was written in just two parts, of which the second, on comedy, was presumably deemed so unimportant as to have been completely lost. Legal orators and their oratorical devices were very well known, written about and circulated before the first extant dramatic evidence comes to our attention. It is unthinkable, I would then propose, to 'think the actor' without the already and everywhere evident advocate. This realignment of cause and effect that I began with, the 'legal act' and '*the act* of law', complicates any simple consequential relationship between theatre and law I might have started out with.

I am not going to call these the 'ten commandments' of the relations between theatre and law, but if I were, it would at least remind us before finishing the first part of this book that before Common Law, which I have referred to so far as though there were no alternative, there was Divine Law.

In the cultures I am considering, that is Common Law cultures, the law 'left' this religious domain in its steady, but only ever partial, secularization. Law apparently left 'faith' and 'belief' behind through the conduct of profane performances that were responsible for securing its efficacious functioning on the side of 'rationality' and 'reason'. Norman Mailer was proved right in this sense at least. The demonic world of *The Crucible* was no longer to hold sway; rather, the family tragedy of the Proctors becomes a study in the improper conduct of human relations borne out within codes and rights.

In encountering the oath earlier, this continuous complication of a dark side is writ large, or spoken loud, in its other: the curse. As Giorgio Agamben says: 'What the curse sanctions is the loosening of the correspondence between words and things that is in question in the oath. If the connection that unites language and the world is broken, the name of God, which expressed and guaranteed this connection in blessing, [*bene-dicente*], becomes the name of the curse [*male-dizione*], that is, of a word that has broken its true relation to things' (2011, p. 42). This 'break' is not only therefore the turbulent sphere in which law is being played out today, but it has always been precisely the 'cursed' ground on which theatre plays its special part. A word that has broken its 'true relation to things' is a word that is spoken in the theatre. The very act of theatricality sunders any necessary causal relation between words and things. That is the a *priori* of all performance. Performance has always been the place where such slippages are no longer there to be forgiven, or not, but to be witnessed for what they reveal to us about the relations between action and intention, effects and affects. So let us go back to the courtroom to see what it has to say about that theatrical act, before we go to the theatre to see what it says about its legal cousin.

part two: before the law: the life and death of '*Homo Juridicus*'

On 5 February 2014 I found myself in Court 5 of the Royal Courts of Justice on Strand in London. In the High Court of Justice, Queen's Bench Division Administrative Court, The Honourable Justice Thirlwall DBE was 'handing down' a judgment in the case of The Queen (On the Application of Mr Steven Earl), the Appellant, and Winchester Crown Court, the Respondent. Unlike some of the very 'dramatic' cases I had witnessed in this place over the last decade, such as the appeal against extradition of the radical cleric Abu Hamza Al-Masri, the inquest over the death of Diana, Princess of Wales, the Dale Farm Travellers' appeal against eviction, or the notorious Mark Duggan shooting enquiry, this judgment was, to all appearances, relatively modest in its effects, though, as we shall soon see, costly for the appellant who lost his case. The judgment also offered a strict definition in law as to who may, or may not, be considered a 'student'.

27

The court hearing had already taken place on 21 and 22 January, and I had not seen anything of it. The judgment had been 'handed down' by Justice Thirlwall to the court clerk below, who in turn handed it to me. It summed up the facts of the case with precision:

> In September 2010 the appellant enrolled on a 2 year full time course leading to a Diploma in Higher Education in Contemporary Performance and Drama studies at the University of Winchester … He failed a double module at the end of his first year. He was permitted to retake that module over the course of the academic year 2011 to 2012 … In the event he completed the module successfully and went on to complete the second year of the diploma in his third year of study. He is now undertaking a degree course … In September 2011 the appellant enrolled at the university. During the early part of the academic year the Council informed him that he was being treated as a part time student and was liable to council tax. In a well argued e mail sent on 15th December 2011 the appellant explained why this was an error and he should be considered a full time student. (Thirlwall, 2014, pp. 4–5)

The crux of the case lay here. A part-time student in the UK would not be considered for local authority tax relief, while a full-time student would. The financial difference such relief might make to a student without resources would be significant, and, indeed, in the case of the appellant it made *all* the difference to his continuation in Higher Education study. The subsequent eight pages of the judgment laid out Justice Thirlwall's reasons for dismissing the appeal and upholding the Council's right to charge Council Tax in the circumstances. While broadly sympathetic to the appellant (the student), the judgment is critical of the university (at one point describing the institution as 'inconsistent', about as damning a judgment as one might imagine from the forensically logical purview of a judge) and in summary appears to count out any contribution it had made to the arguments, with the quietly crushing rider:

> Both parties agreed that the position of the university is not determinative of whether the student was a student within the meaning of the legislation at the material time. I agree. In the circumstances I propose to ignore the contradictory evidence from the university. (p. 6)

Contrary to one's expectation that it would be a university in 21st-century Britain that might have a defining role in determining the status and identity of a university student, here Justice Thirlwall would appear to be departing from any such presumption. By implication, the rest of the judgment appears to suggest it might be other conditions that should be taken into account when considering what defines a student. And here Justice Thirlwall is discussing the definition of a theatre student. In a final section, confidently subtitled by the judge 'The Correct approach' (this is how it is capitalized in the judgment as though to emphasize the Correctness of what we are about to read, as distinct to its 'approach-ness'), it is concluded that whatever other arguments have been proposed, what the appellant has been involved in is indeed 'not a full time course of education' and that 'notwithstanding the careful and detailed argument presented by both counsel that is where the case begins and ends' (p. 9). The judgment concludes: 'At the material time the appellant was not enrolled to undertake a full time course of education. He was not therefore a student within the meaning of the Regulation 4 and paragraph 4 of Schedule 1 to the Local Government and Finance Act 1992. He was therefore liable to pay council tax' (p. 10).

The convoluted tale of Mr Steven Earl, the disappointment of his theatre module failures, his subsequent renaissance following successful retakes, his entry to a degree programme, his loss of financial relief from the local council, is a narrative that would be well known to students studying across the UK, and perhaps other countries, where educational support systems include significant and much-needed secondary benefits such as subsidized accommodation. What lifts Mr Earl's case out from the common run of others is his tenacity to take this case, and the cause it represents, to appeal in the second highest court in the land. It is in a way the quintessential 'small' yet practical politics of the 21st century student. It is now no longer a question of attendance at court for 'criminal' damage perpetrated in the resistance to Apartheid, no longer the civil disobedience case following the tagging of nuclear missiles at Greenham Common, no longer 'illegal' trespass on the property of an environment despoiling multi-corporation. Rather, in Mr Earl's case, it is the important principle that one gets one's just recognition as a 'student' in the Local Government and Finance Act of 1992. And that is what Mr Earl failed to achieve. This apparent modesty is what attracted me to this case as an exemplar of the common conduct of the law, as perhaps distinct to its more obviously 'theatrical' character when the names (and liberties) of OJ Simpson, Amanda Knox and Oscar Pistorius are in the dock. And, as with the other examples in this book, it has the benefit of an act (albeit a legal one) I have experienced *directly*, which is how I like to keep it when it comes to commentating on theatrical experience.

At the opening of this section I say I 'found myself' through this judgment, partly because it alerted me to the continuous and complex way the law, an intangible phenomena after all, determines the very preconditions for the definition and, indeed perhaps, as in Mr Earl's case, existence of any 'student'. For any student who might read this, your very precariousness or security presumably rests on such cases. And, on the other hand, this experience drew my attention to the way that it is precisely the 'theatre', albeit in this legal narrative in the form of an education course claiming to know what theatre 'is' and therefore legitimately qualified to engage people who become students in its study, that hovers throughout the action as a second, indeterminate point of reference that never quite gets defined but shapes everything that takes place.

And I say I found myself on that morning in 2014 because the *affects* of this case, as became apparent in discussing its merits in the corridor afterwards with the representative official attending on behalf of Winchester Council, manifested themselves as feelings of disappointment (for the student), laughter (at the university's incoherent paper work), admiration (for the prose style and broad humanity of the judgment despite its harsh conclusions) and unease and anxiety (as to what it might mean for others, those who followed Mr Earl with their disappointing 'module outcomes'). This was an occasion, despite its melancholic banality, full of affects, in other words emotions and feelings, one might associate more commonly with a heightened theatre event, while the effects of the legal case were all too obvious for the losing party and seemed to take second place to these more immediate, human responses. And it was an occasion whose consequences, despite their legitimacy and rightness in law, seemed, to me at least, wholly 'wrong' in the world.

The valley to the waterers

In the case of performance I might have thought before that morning's judgment that *affects* (or feelings) were all, while in the case of law, *effects* (or consequences) were all. Surely, in the end, whatever I might have to say about theatre and law in this book, it is law that has to make a difference, while performance, despite any higher aspirations I might have for it, has no responsibility whatsoever to change anything.

Of course, any familiarity with theatre history of the 20th century in general, and the work of numerous theatre makers from Bertolt Brecht to Augusto Boal, would bring any such supposition of a simple bifurcation between theatre and law on these grounds into question, a complication I am happy to entertain as I proceed through the coming pages.

Indeed my own experiences as a student in the mid 1970s should have reminded me of this more complicated relation between theatre and law, and they were not that far removed from Mr Earl's and his engagement with the presiding judge, Justice Thirlwall. I too was busy failing modules (at school, having started to fail earlier than Mr Earl) when I found myself caught up in the public staging of the representation of a legal process whose form was meant to propagate political effects, when in fact it was affects that saturated my memory of the experience.

I had been cast, by an enduringly optimistic mathematics teacher who had first-hand experience of my innumeracy, in the role of Azdak the Judge in Bertolt Brecht's play *Der Kaukasische Kreidekreis* (1942), translated by Eric Bentley as: *The Caucasian Chalk Circle* (1975). The drunken, lecherous layman, Azdak, has a remarkable, and not wholly deleterious, impact on his community for someone who has essentially donned the robes of law out of expediency. This 'village scrivener' turned magistrate sums up the relations between ceremony and legal identity: 'it would be easier for a judge's robe and a judge's hat to pass judgment than for a man with no robe and no hat. If you don't treat it with respect, the law just disappears on you' (Brecht, p. 180).

Azdak appears in the latter half of the play, which has been framed at the outset from the perspective of a pair of competing Russian communes where the retreating Nazi forces in the late days of World War II have left a landscape of disputation over the rights to farm. Through a series of mock trials and counter-intuitive, if commonsensical, judgments, Azdak gains the preferment of the Grand Duke, who, at the cusp of his hanging, pardons Azdak and invests him with judicial power. But Azdak has for some time, inadvertently but effectively, been the 'judge at large' in this war-torn place. This subsequent, second order of investiture is met with a paradoxical retort by the Ironshirt, whose office requires him to officiate over such matters of appointment: 'I beg to report that His Honour Azdak was already His Honour Azdak.' Thus, essentially, by the end of the play from whence he slips away unnoticed, with no apparent identity and having lost a double identity, Azdak has *become himself* through the processes of law.

I too had somehow lost an identity while apparently gaining one. While I appeared to have played the part of Azdak in the long final act, *The Chalk Circle*, at least according to the cast list in the lavishly (and painstakingly) Gestetnered programme, the role had been played in the longer, and dramatically more significant, penultimate act, 'The Story of the Judge', by someone else entirely, with a similar but typographically inept name – 'Alan Reid', with an 'i' not an 'a'. You can check how it is meant to be on the cover of this book. I remember quite forcefully the retrospective anxiety this modest secretarial mishap caused me at the time, and on reflection it has an acute legal dimension that I could not have been aware of.

This administrative detail, this paperwork, is wholly in keeping with Brecht's own dramaturgy in this particular play. Despite the way Azdak is often played as a complete legal outsider, he is nothing of the sort. In the very introduction of the character, Brecht described him in the following way: 'The Village Scrivener Azdak found a fugitive in the woods and hid him in his hut.' While he might be simple of means he is not without his own expertise, and that is a legal expertise. A scrivener (or scribe) was after all a person who could read and write, copied legal documents or wrote letters to court.

What I understood then about law I learned through playing that part of a scrivener turned law-maker, not really by any other familiarity with law's systems. I learned that because, in playing that part of a judge, I began to recognize that assuming this role really did not mark quite the difference I might have expected to have been obvious between my legal identity, my theatrical 'legal' role and my extra-legal identity that the stage offered. In other words in the same order, I noticed a contamination between my status as a student threatened with exclusion, my conduct in the role of Azdak the renegade judge and the temporary immunity, a theatrical *cordon sanitaire*, from imminent school discipline and sanction that this accident of casting offered me.

Entering the law via the theatrical logic of the stage, costumed in this way, it occurred to me it was as if *this* law, the one I, as Azdak, was busy dispensing, was already peculiarly familiar to me as a performer. I did not need to know the famous line by the ethnographer Clifford Geertz, that law 'is part of a distinct manner of imagining the real' (1983, p. 173), to recognize the fundamental link between a legal sensibility and a performance sensibility that is also dedicated to representing that same 'reality' in its own fashion. If law imagines a 'real', then performance is certainly another 'show business' that trades on such 'reals'. I was, you could say, born to, and made for, such a legal role, and I would here, with the confidence of the work of anthropologists behind me, contend that we all are. It is as though law in this form had somehow always been present in my life, and that without knowing anything about law or legal process, I was already deeply familiar with what it should, or might, be. You could say I was already born to, and bound by, the law. As such, from infancy on, I would suggest I am less 'Homer Faber', the human who works, or 'Homo Ludens', the human who plays, but rather 'Homo Juridicus', the human who is lawful. A figure 'full' of law, from the inside as well as out.

To explore these relations between legal identity and human 'being', as I want to do here, will require a brief detour via some quite large questions that other, longer books would dwell at length upon and yet probably still give the feeling of having been summarily dispatched. There is a serious thread in the anthropology of law that suggests that it is legal concepts 'within a jural community that define community structure. They allow the establishment of relationships' (Pirie, p. 53). In other words, it is from precisely such a symbolic grammar as that of law that an idea of reality might be constructed. Definitions of property and ownership through law would be the most obvious example of such definitions, ones which indeed impact very directly on those questions of land ownership at the heart of Brecht's play. As Geertz has said, law provides 'visions of a community, not echoes of it' (1983, p. 218). But beyond ownership, questions of contract, trust, responsibility, guilt and personality are also at stake though law, as the sociologist Roger Cotterrell has suggested, and in this sense 'law provides a model for how society can be' (Pirie, p. 53).

Alain Supiot, the French ethnographer of law, goes one further and offers a particularly detailed reading of this anthropological thread that binds us to law, which would seem to connect most directly to my own theatrical example (2007). He reminds us that human beings are not born rational but they *become* so by gaining access to meaning shared with others. If we are to enjoy thinking and expressing ourselves freely in language, we must first submit to the limits that give words meaning. This would seem to be the most obvious lesson one might learn from reading a court judgment such as that of *Earl vs Winchester City Council* considered earlier.

But, before I arrived at my own awareness of my being through speech, I had already been named and situated within a lineage, a lineage that went by the name of 'Read', as in 'to read the riot act', not 'Reid' (as printed in that programme) or indeed any other name. A place was assigned to me within a succession of generations by this naming, not just within the hierarchy of a theatrical cast list. I take it from this postnatal anecdote that before we can dispose of ourselves freely and say 'I', we are already a subject of law, bound, *subjectum*, thrown under, by words, names and language, which tie us to others. It is through such processes, Supiot suggests, that the bonds of law and the bonds of speech converge, enabling every newborn child to become a member of humanity, to have his or her life endowed with recognized meaning.

If the insurrection-torn opening scenes of *The Caucasian Chalk Circle* are about anything they put into play this dilemma. A child, Michael, born of the governing class, the Abashwillis, is abandoned by his mother, the Governor's wife (preoccupied with saving her wardrobe) and is saved from the marauding Ironshirts by a farm girl, Grusha, with the peasant name Vashnadze. Almost unwittingly, but with the instinct of care that escapes the Governor's wife, Grusha picks up the abandoned child and flees in protection of his young life.

Law is a rule, but it is also a command that is granted by an authority that is empowered to enact it. In the state of exception that characterizes the opening of *The Caucasian Chalk Circle*, the norms associated with this higher power, the authority of the law, have collapsed into a chaos of local determinations wrought through violence. Those who are weak within such a chaos, and Grusha the farm girl is weak because she has no power within this regime and not because she lacks strength (that much is evident from her courageous peripatetic journey through the first half of the play and its threatening landscapes), are prey to the vicissitudes of the sovereign power that in the scene that follows the opening insurrection of the play is conceived between an unholy alliance of aristocracy and banditry. *The Caucasian Chalk Circle* is a play that by its closure reconstitutes the law at its most primal, as 'an expression of general will', where 'right' means 'just'. Here a form of natural law that Azdak conducts is staged and made sufficiently public for those who hear it and become subject to it, to take on its obligations. In a Christian context these rights would commonly be secured with reference to a higher order of God, but in this post-war Marxist state, a simpler expedient prevails in which those who will care for things (waterers in the instance of the valley in question) will take responsibility for their protection and growth.

Supiot suggests it is by transforming each of us into a *Homo Juridicus* through such processes that the biological and symbolic dimensions that make up our being have been linked together. That is, in the West at least. For Supiot is diligent in his separation of juridical process in those cultures that do not subscribe to the Western legal canon, and he sees some hope for the reformation of law and the future of humankind precisely in those other traditions. It is precisely the *law*, Supiot suggests, that connects our infinite mental universe, all life's possibilities in the radical heteronomy of all possible actions, with our finite, limited, actual physical existence, and in so doing fulfils the anthropological function of instituting us as rational beings. In this sense we are recognizable *as* human beings, precisely because we are legal beings first. It is this 'first', a priori claim law makes on us that marks us as *Homo Juridicae*.

This affirmative narrative brings forcefully to mind one
of the lessons that Hannah Arendt draws from the experience of totalitarianism, published just before the first production of *The Caucasian Chalk Circle* in Germany in the
early 1950s, where she says: 'The first essential step on the
road to total domination is to kill the *juridical person*' (1967,
p. 477, my emphasis). So, while for Supiot it is *Homo Juridicus*
that secures personhood in 'a life', it is the extermination
of *Homo Juridicus* that turns that person into a superfluous
being, or 'extraneous person', as I will demonstrate in the
final section of this book.

To *deny* the anthropological function of the law in the
name of a supposed 'realism' grounded in biology, politics
or economics is something that all totalitarian projects have
in common. This lesson, Supiot believes, seems to have
been forgotten by the jurists who today argue, in the interests of 'human rights' even, that the legal person is a 'pure
construct' bearing no relation to the concrete human being.
The legal person in this world view commonly character-
ized as the 'postmodern condition' is just that, a construct.
But in the symbolic universe that we inhabit according
to the postmodernists, that is our lot – everything is, of
course, a construct. We are all performers now. In other
words, legal personality in this world view is, contra my
argument so far, certainly *not* a fact of nature but rather
a certain *representation* of the human being. And *if* it is a
representation, and not a fact of nature, then while legal
identity might constitute part of our anthropological make-
up as human beings, it is an identity, from the outset, that

operates through investitures that might well be theatrical (as in my casting as Azdak) but are also, and everywhere, performative. Our legal being is thus constructed in ways that could, for instance, be structurally related to our gendered being, precisely performatively, as suggested by Judith Butler in her formative work, *Gender Trouble* (1990).

But such playfulness with gender and legal identity does not, for Brecht at least, begin in the relative freedoms of the North American university campus; it starts unevenly in material historical conditions of inequality and dissensus as to the right to even claim such a freedom *to* self-identity. Rights can be repealed as easily as secured where performative investitures are concerned. As the writer and theatre practitioner Rustom Bharucha once said to me in a personal conversation when he heard me spout the platitude that 'we' must 'reclaim the right to performance': 'Who is in a position, political, legal, economic or social, to do such reclaiming?' and 'How precisely might such reclaiming occur for those historically excluded from any such "right"?' It is precisely in the wake of the totalitarian history of the 20th century, the totalitarian history that provides the very starting point for Brecht's play in which the Kolkhoz villagers are debating the distribution of lands following the retreat of the Nazis from their war-ravaged landscape, that it was deemed necessary to extend legal personality and the prohibition it contains to every 'person' wherever they may be. It is this prohibition that is really being challenged, Supiot makes clear, when people today seek to disqualify the subject of law and treat the human

41

being as a mere accounting unit, like a commodity or, more or less the same thing, as an abstraction.

While Supiot helpfully emphasizes linguistic aspects of shared symbolic meanings, he underestimates visual signs and representations critical to the relations between theatre and law. All systems of law are according to Peter Goodrich 'lived and presenced' through codified clusters of icons, images and symbols. Hence the need for an ontology of the law as I have been proposing, and also a recognition of those discursive practices that give humans access to the meaning of such signs as laid out in the first section of this book. This is quite obvious to Paul Raffield, who emphasizes the ways in which the English Common Law tradition precisely operates without any 'textual codification' to secure it (2007).

The *Homo Juridicus* that is 'us', I am suggesting, then operates within a law that is made up of a complex of human conditions that might be described as anthropological in character, but importantly also through a repertoire of visually inscribed performative operations that clothe these conditions. These performative operations might appear not just in the form of costuming, as in Azdak's case, but also in ceremonial processes of investiture and acclamation, ritual conduct and belief. I take it that bringing these narratives together, ethnographic and performative, representational and iconographic, and exploring the consequence of their meeting has been part of my task in writing this essay. I will take this further in the third part of this book with regards to the crisis for human identity that ensues when such apparatuses fail to operate in the interests of human justice.

In that Brecht play that so disorientated me, the chalk circle drawn upon the ground in which the final trial of strength for the child takes place was, after all, *an image* born of myth (the judgment of Solomon in the bible where two women claim the same child). At the end of the play, the chalk circle and its magical arena of justice does not survive the transition back into the world of work, where the valley must 'go to the waterers, that it yield fruit'. The rogue judge after all does not so much take leave of this community as *waste away* at the moment of its coerced coming together, like the chalk on the ground. As Azdak takes off his robe for the last time he 'invites' those present, whose tribulations he has solved with a sequence of improvised judgments, to 'a little dance in the meadow outside'. As he signs the final divorce papers for the wrong couple, the dance music is heard. Azdak cannot withdraw his final clerical error, an error of office, because as he says: 'If I did how could we keep order in the land?' Azdak 'stands lost in thought. The dancers soon hide him from view. Occasionally he is seen, but less and less as more couples join the dance.' The Singer who has narrated the story of the chalk circle wraps up the occasion: 'And after that evening Azdak vanished and was never seen again. / The people of Grusinia did not forget him but long remembered / The period of his judging as a brief golden age. / Almost an age of justice.' The best law has to offer, in keeping with what has gone before, is still not 'quite' justice. As the couples dance, Brecht's stage directions are enigmatic, but decisive – Azdak has 'disappeared'. The director's note to me before the opening night of that school production was, I recall, something like: 'Find a way to disappear from view without attracting attention to yourself.' This was not how it was, nor how it could be, theatrically at least. I recall attracting more, not less, attention to myself as I tried unsuccessfully to dissimulate. The recalcitrance of my body 'in law' as well as 'in performance', its resistance to being summarily disappeared by a stage direction, might be at least partly explained with recourse to the legal bodies of Franz Kafka's work.

In The Penal Colony

I am at the Young Vic, a theatre in South London, it is 2011, and Palestinian company ShiberHur are presenting their theatrical version of Kafka's short story *In The Penal Colony* (1914, 2005). A prisoner, about to be executed, has been laid out on an apparatus by an officer who is answerable to an offstage commandant who has superseded the superior who perfected this legal machine. An explorer has come across this world of summary justice in a parched valley on an island with only the sun above and no other witnesses to the action. There were once, we discover later, huge audiences for such public events of correction, but in recent times viewers for this legal spectacle have collapsed, and we are in the dog days of recrimination. The officer seeks a supporter for the effectiveness of his procedures, and the explorer is drawn into witnessing a demonstration of the machine's continued relevance and worth.

The officer draws a chair to the lip of a pit in which the machine sits. He gestures to the explorer to take his place.

The 'remarkable apparatus', as the officer introduces it to the explorer (its only rather ominous drawback is that it 'gets so messy'), has three parts, clearly visible to us in the auditorium that makes up the Young Vic – the Bed, the Designer and the Harrow. The condemned man is laid out on the Bed covered in absorbent cotton wool, face down and gagged, while the Harrow, a ribbon of steel, shuttles between the Designer, the frame that hangs above the prisoner's body. Battery powered, the bed begins to quiver in concert with the Harrow, which is described by the officer as the instrument for the actual execution of the sentence: 'Whatever commandment the prisoner has disobeyed is written upon his body by the Harrow. This prisoner, for instance' – the officer indicated the man – 'will have written on his body: HONOR THY SUPERIORS' (2005, p. 144).

Kafka hovers authorially somewhere beyond this narrative as it is being dramatically rendered, and he spectrally appears in the form of his text, translated, in the streaming English surtitles above the action. I obviously cannot presume that the humans in this scene follow Alain Supiot's foundational, ontological rules of shared and symbolic meanings, for here the language of the officer is not understood by the prisoner (who cannot know the nature or duration of his sentence), nor does he know a sentence has even been passed upon him. The officer emphasizes: 'There would be no point in telling him. He'll learn it on his body' (p. 145). And, of course, given that he knows neither his sentence nor that he has *been* sentenced, he cannot offer any defence as to his innocence. In this world where executioner is also judge, 'guilt is never to be doubted' (p.146). It does not take a theologian to offer religious interpretations of these lines.

But this, as the explorer is aware, is a 'penal colony'. We also know this because we might know the title of Kafka's story or, indeed, we have booked tickets for a show with just this name. And as Kafka says, a penal colony is where 'extraordinary measures were needed and that military discipline must be enforced to the last' (p. 146). You might say, after the political theorist Carl Schmitt, that this is a 'state of exception' (*Ausnahmetzustand*) in which a government has extended its juridical powers in a time of supposed crisis. Here, individual rights are surrendered in the wake of extensions of state power. And it is these extraordinary measures, in this place, that require performance to do their work for them: 'the Harrow is lowered onto the body. It regulates itself automatically so that the needles barely touch the skin … And then the performance begins. An ignorant onlooker would see no difference between one punishment and another … And now anyone can look through the glass and watch the inscription taking form on the body' (2005, p. 147).

The blood flowing from the inscription is channelled away down a wastepipe into the pit as the explorer looks on. The cotton wool is staunching the bleeding for now and allows for the 'deepening of the script' over time (we are told 6–12 hours on average). Once 'enlightenment', or perhaps more accurately from Kafka's German, 'understanding', has been achieved, the body is pitched from the saturated bed. Here the writing machine of the law has to be prepared in such a way as to calibrate the death of the subject in only those stages that allow for the completion of the law's message. But this method of execution has lost its adherents in the colony, and the officer is seeking a way to protect his professional purpose. He has found himself, perhaps ironically, in the place of the Kafkaesque outsider in a world in which he once acted as judge, juror and justice. In his paranoia he suspects the new commandant has invited the explorer to witness the event to reveal its redundancy: 'you will see that the execution has no support from the public, a shabby ceremony – carried out with a machine already somewhat old and worn' (p. 155).

The officer suspects that the explorer has been invited to compare his own culture's more enlightened machineries of justice with those of this barbaric state. But the explorer insists that he has no view to offer, given he is an outsider and has no intention of entering into a debate as to the merits, or not, of this foreign justice system. The officer, devastated by the loss of the last witness to his life's cause, releases the condemned man, clambers onto the Bed and subjects himself to the machinery while the condemned man witnesses the procedure with fascinated awe. The apparatus runs amok, haywire, jabbing irrationally and spasmodically at the officer in torrents of blood. If the prisoner has just been subjected to the language of the law, then the officer is in turn subjected to the pure violence of the law. Subsequently, the explorer, the officer and the condemned man reconvene in a morgue-like teahouse where the commandant's tomb marks his earlier demise – and theirs. But the explorer is able to leave across a river, something like the Styx, in which he repels the reaching hands of those he leaves behind on the far side. There is no clemency here despite his apparent compassion.

The final scene is from Kafka, not from ShiberHur's performance at the Young Vic. But the 'flesh and bones' of the occasion are there in the balance of the summary I have offered. What is not there in this rather literary rendering is the *theatrical* sense and impact that this peculiar legal scene makes on any spectator who might be remotely sensitive to the politics of the state from which ShiberHur have come to present their work to a cosmopolitan London audience. It is important to reiterate, given the significance of language to law as I have laid out so far, that this production is one that I am witnessing in London but am listening to in Arabic, a language I do not understand, with the benefit of surtitles in English, when I wish to look at them.

ShiberHur was founded in 2009 in Haifa by Amir Nizar Zuabi, Amer Hlehel, Ali Sliman, Ashraf Hanna and Ruba Billal. It is Zuabi who directs Hlehel in *In The Penal Colony* with Makram J Khoury and Taher Najib in the other roles. When one considers that Shiber Hur means something like 'an inch of freedom' (from an Ottoman measuring unit equivalent to an open palm), that this company's work has toured previously to Palestinian refugee camps in the West Bank and Galilee, and that it has involved work directly relating through domestic means to the events of partition in 1948 in *I am Yusuf and This is My Brother* (Young Vic, 2010), one cannot watch the foregoing apparatus of legal inscription as anything but a commentary on the current conditions of the company operating from within the tensions of the Middle East conflict. In their previous work at this venue, *I am Yusuf*, it is the daily routines of life that are the centre of the theatrical experience and from which the wider sense of the Arab-Israeli war (*al Nakba*, 'the Catastrophe' as Palestinians consider the events of 1948) is construed through a personal relationship of prohibition. If that was a 'small play' in political terms, as Zuabi describes it in his programme note, then *In The Penal Colony* is a big play, politically revealing the machineries of terror and the state, of legislation and persecution, and of state control and violence.

The performance operates as an extended meditation on the violence of the law, as Walter Benjamin construed it in his seminal work 'Critique of Violence' (2002). And, importantly for the purposes of this book, it does this through specifically theatrical means. This is not to say for a moment that Kafka's narrative has not solicited as many readings as there are readers, from analyses that perceive the two commandants as exemplars of the 'God of Orthodox Judaism' and 'Reform Judaism' (Steinberg, 1976) to the mobilization of the figure of the penal colony as the exemplar for capital punishment in its relation to the philosophy of the law (Sitze, 1999). But I would contend here it is only because this is a performance, in public, that the work operates at the 'level' it does, by which I mean combining striking effects as well as profound affects. I say this not because I consider theatre to be an unusually persuasive social or political medium; I have made clear in other work where any such presumption might be questioned quite critically in this age of multiple social platforms and media screens (Read, 2008). I say this rather because of the inherent anthropological and ontological connections between theatre and law I have just been considering, and because of the principles of performativity that allow legal process to operate that I laid out in the ten associations between theatre and law in the first section of the book.

If Carlo Galli in his work *Political Spaces and Global War* (2010) is right and all political thought has an 'implicit spatiality', then the penal colony, as it is theatrically represented (that is, through design and construction) by ShiberHur, becomes the scene for that spatial engagement. The political space of *this* setting, the one before me on the stage of the Young Vic, stands for another setting as though by proxy or surrogate, which the audience are not asked to imagine but which nevertheless appears as the production proceeds, and that is a spatial setting which has been striated and severed by history. This space is not the passive container of the politics and law that take their place there, it is the *active,* contested space that generates these very conditions of participation and exclusion from political process in the Palestinian/Israeli conflict.

But recall now that the final scene of the officer's engagement with his beloved machine is one of *suicide*. He places *himself* in the contraption and initiates his own end as well as that of his beloved machine, which unravels spectacularly around him. In a gloss on Galli's work, Adam Sitze persuasively argues that in so doing it is the death penalty itself that is being put to death (Sitze, p. 241). Until this point, remember, the officer is not an executioner but a murderer. It is only with his *own* death that his role as executioner becomes appropriate – he is the first party who is guilty of the crime that might, on any logical legal grounds founded in a rational legal system, necessitate this death machine. Here, a form of justice has been seen to prevail in a manifestly unjust universe. It is only on reading and understanding the inscription on the Commandant's tomb, in the tea room, the first inscription and text that the explorer has understood in this place, that the explorer realizes that it is not just the apparatus he has been witnessing that is at stake here, but the state as a whole that is the installation, the apparatus or, indeed, the machine.

One is left in no doubt in this production that while the penal colony is *not* a metaphor for the Palestine/Israel conflict, it does demark something of the spatiality of the legalization of death that has been so fiendishly omnipresent within that conflict. Sitze points out that it is neither in visiting the colony nor in escaping it that the demonic machine of legal violence can be deactivated, but rather in 'abiding in it' with what he calls 'probity and persistence' (p. 248). In a sense this is what the durational aspect of the theatrical immersion in this law machine offers. It offers the opportunity in time to abide in something one might not have expected, nor perhaps have particularly wanted. In such 'abiding', no one in ShiberHur nor the Young Vic is implying that there is a commensurate engagement, or equivalence of experience, with those who are occupied and tyrannized elsewhere. But both do suggest by invitation to participate that *some* form of affinity with the subjects of this action, Arabic-speaking Palestinians after all, is enacted in any such engagement within theatrical time and space.

We nevertheless do leave the island in the end, under the green EXIT sign that indicates to us the appropriately named street outside the Young Vic, The Cut. And we exit via a ceramic-tiled butchers'-shop-cum-foyer that remains the only surviving structure in this part of the street of a massive wartime bomb that marks this location out as its own site of historical conflict. One would have to presume, if one's theatrical imagination is at all alive, that we leave behind us somewhere in the auditorium, between the world of the play and the offstage world to which it signals, the condemned man, who is innocent. He has been abandoned already, at least theatrically, by the explorer, and now we cosmopolitan believers in 'justice for all' abandon him *in the theatre*, for real. Of course one is always asked to 'leave behind' those who retreat to the dressing room. But we are not always quite so conscious that the home of those just 'retreated' from public view is under imminent threat. It is an exit, from the stage for the subjected and the auditorium for witnesses, that is troubling at just about every level theatre and law might mutually offer, a mutuality that *is* the point. In the final section of this book I will demonstrate how these subjects of 'legal' violence are themselves part of a growing community of those who have something in common, becoming superfluous in legal terms and through legal means.

part three: beyond the law: extraordinary rendition

I said I 'found myself' through law in the second part of this book, and I want to finish by looking at ways in which people 'lose themselves' through law and how performance and image making might remind us of such losses and their consequences. On 15 March 1982, I was sitting in the Public Gallery of the Old Bailey in London, witnessing the trial of the theatre director Michael Bogdanov, who had been served a writ by the solicitor for the moral majoritarian and President of the National Viewers and Listeners' Association, Mary Whitehouse, under the Sexual Offences Act of 1956. The writ accused him of 'having procured an act of gross indecency by [the actors] Peter Sproule with Greg Hicks on the stage of the Olivier Theatre'. Putting on a play, *The Romans in Britain* (1980), thus became commensurate in the conduct of this law with soliciting sex. What Bogdanov thought he had done, and those of us who had seen Howard Brenton's play at the National Theatre in December 1980 thought he had done (and Whitehouse never saw the play on the logical grounds that it would morally deprave her), was direct a scene set in 54 BCE in which Sproule, playing the part of a Celt called Marban, and Hicks, playing the part of an invading Roman called Third Soldier, pretended to have sex. They had in fact been simulating anal rape since the opening in October 1980, until 19 December, when the solicitor viewed the production and served the writ. It did not take much political awareness to notice the contemporary allusions to colonial invasion and the Irish question that were central to the play, and as though to ensure there was no doubt as to this symmetry, in the latter part of the production a tank rolls across the stage, bringing the audience into the contemporary world of Ulster politics.

In the well of the court I saw Ian Kennedy QC, on behalf of Whitehouse and the prosecution, argue that obscenity was obscenity whether in a theatre or on a street. In defence of Bogdanov in turn, it was argued that law could not be used against the stage in this way, not least of all because no sex took place, rather it was the theatrical simulation of sex. The solicitor who was called on behalf of the prosecution, who had acted as the proxy audience member on behalf of Whitehouse, insisted under cross-examination that he had seen 'the tip of the penis' of the actor playing the Third Soldier. But when presented with a seating plan of the Olivier Theatre auditorium, and asked by the defence lawyer Geoffrey Robertson to mark where he had sat, his cross was placed in the last row of the stalls, a full 100 feet from the action. As anyone would know who had tried to see plays in that vast, quasi-Greek auditorium, one would need something more than 20/20 vision to see anything of the sort from there. Either that or Hicks was in the wrong 'oldest profession'. While the ensuing dramatization of what could or could not be seen – it was in fact a fist and a thumb that had so 'offended the solicitor' – provoked constrained laughter in the court, there was a lasting, and serious, side to the botched outcome. The presiding judge ruled that the 1956 Sexual Offences Act *could* be applied to the theatre, but almost immediately Kennedy, on behalf of the prosecution, withdrew from the case, telling the court: 'The consequences of conviction – irrespective of penalty – would greatly damage Mr Bogdanov in his personal and professional life.' I recall the somewhat selfish feeling of disappointment that those of us present were not going to get a judgment either way, an almost unique situation in English law, without the prospect of a retrial. An official of the Queen was instead sent to court to offer the plea of *nolle prosequi*: no prosecution.

While this episode would appear to have no lasting impact on those involved, though Mary Whitehouse rather hopefully commented that 'God' would 'pay her costs', my understanding of the legal situation at the close of the trial was that Bogdanov was never formally acquitted, the case having been closed down leaving the accused in an unusual state of suspension. Given the play *The Romans in Britain* was itself the dramatization of a state of exception in which the violent rule of a colonial force, the Romans, meted out 'justice' to those indigenous people, the Celts and Druids, who got in their way, there was something at least symmetrical in this suspended judgment. In the case of the Celts in 54 BCE, a way to have described their value for the occupying forces might have been 'superfluous persons', and in his own way, the director Michael Bogdanov became himself a surrogate form of such a 'superfluous person' in the suspended judgment against him. It is almost certainly not coincidental that *The Romans in Britain*, despite, in my recollection, being one of the finest British plays of its generation, and indeed one of the *only* plays I recall that reflected upon the Irish question through a panoramic dramatic imaginary, was itself suspended from the UK theatre repertoire, only receiving its next revival at the Crucible Theatre, Sheffield under the direction of Sam West in 2006, a full quarter century after its first, troubled staging. Not only had this play therefore become superfluous, its author, Howard Brenton, also suffered a period of apparent isolation from the theatre world he had illuminated with plays such as *Magnificence* (1973) and *The Churchill Play* (1974), a period that has perhaps been adjusted for now given his prodigious later work. As Helen Freshwater has made clear in her comprehensive study, it is the complex 'heterogeneity of censorship' that demands attention in such instances, not just some preordained presumption of State-sponsored rectitude over the so-called 'freedoms of the artist' (Freshwater, 2009).

It should not be forgotten then, in this context, that amongst such persons subjected to law are people who call themselves, or are referred to by others as 'artists'.

Given work I have done elsewhere in the book *Theatre &
Everyday Life* (1993), on unpicking the presumptions inherent in any such 'artistic' category, I will not retreat here
and unduly privilege such identities amongst the many
others who are marginalized, excluded or disappeared by
legal process. That said, under the Obscene Publications
Act of 1959, in the UK publication of Vladimir Nabokov's
Lolita, D.H. Lawrence's *Lady Chatterley's Lover* and the *Oz*
trials have all contested the rights of artists and authors to
'free expression', while the presence of a book of Robert
Mapplethorpe's photographs in a library in the University
of the West of England 'almost led to the Vice Chancellor of
that University being charged under the 1959 Act' (Kearns,
p. 19). Amidst this litany of repressive attention from the
authorities, it should be remembered that, despite the atten-
tions they 'enjoy', it is not just performance and live artists,
over the last two decades, that have been subjected to the
draconian side of the law when it comes to authoritarian
assaults on identity and personhood. Indeed, these instances
of censorship and threat do have the benefit at least of being
relatively well documented in Freshwater (2009), Kearns
(2013) and the web site *Artquest*, for instance. So, for these
concluding examples, I will reach rather further afield than
the art world itself, while setting out precisely from an artist's engagement with these concerns.

Colin Dayan has catalogued what she calls such 'extraneous persons', subordinated and expelled from society,
and what it means to be considered in terms of a law that
is as likely to diminish as to empower: 'law dwells on,

messes with, and consumes persons. It is through law that persons, variously figured, gain or lose definition, become victims of prejudice or inheritors of privilege. And once outside the valuable discriminations of personhood, their claims become inconsequential' (2011, p. xi). Here I will shift the wilful voluntarism of my analysis of playing Azdak in *The Caucasian Chalk Circle* to the harder realism of 21st-century law under the jurisdiction of states of exception wrought in the wake of al-Qaeda's attacks on the World Trade Center and the Pentagon and the subsequent 'war on terror' [sic]. While Dayan's focus on idioms of servility and State-sanctioned degradation are trenchantly aimed at the US context, legal histories of dispossessions are as readily apparent wherever one looks, though not always with the overt self-dramatization of the debacles of Guantanamo Bay, mass penal servitude in the unusually cruel conditions of solitary confinement, and public executions.

For Dayan, 'negative personhood' describes slaves, animals, criminals and detainees who are, as she says, 'disabled by law' (p. xii). My consideration of negative personhood will embrace those excluded by State legislation, evicted Travellers, and subjects of extraordinary rendition, the contemporary descendants perhaps of those Celts in *The Romans in Britain*. Each incapacitation through 'sinkholes of the law' is a disablement conducted through a performative process. Depersonalization, taking us in the opposite direction of the legal ontology that constitutes human being in the last chapter, disfigures persons in as much as they become subject to law's violence. As Dayan has convincingly demonstrated, it is 'rituals of belief' that attend to, and lubricate, such processes, and amongst such rituals of belief I would suggest theatrical practices play their own part for good, or often ill. Indeed, there are moments and places where such rituals of belief become so entwined with practices of law that the two become imperceptible to the point of complete confusion.

What is shared by the US context and the examples I am going to concentrate briefly upon is that, once returned to their communities, the subjects of these processes are diminished and harmed, sometimes beyond 'repair or redress', as Dayan soberly notes. You could say this section deals with the obverse, or lethal, antidote to the openness of *habeas corpus* considered in the opening pages of this book; it concerns the secretion of the body to a place that one could only describe as a place of 'dark law'. Whatever this place is, by definition in theatrical terms it is obscene, offscene – that is, kept offstage at all costs. Its constant eruption into view, insisting on appearance, is nothing to do with the State and everything to do with courageous individuals, advocates (including artists) who bring due attention to what others would prefer we did not see.

Conditions apply

In keeping with the rest of this book, I would want to open up these troubling occasions through acts of performance and image making, in this instance through the work of the visual artist Carey Young, whose 15-year project (at the time of writing) has taken a serious interest in the law, its effects, and its affects. Unusually, Young has worked with legal experts in constructing a sequence of gallery pieces that do not so much render legal issues visible through means of content (as in *In the Penal Colony*) or representation (as in *The Caucasian Chalk Circle*), but rather implicate the viewer, the gallery visitor and public audience of the work, within the frame of the installation itself, in the form of an immersive encounter with the power of legal concepts.

One of Young's most recent works might usefully connect where I have been and where I am going with this book. In *We the People (after Pierre Cavellat)* (2013), a human-sized photographic work in luscious, glossed colours was installed in *Le Quartier* in Brittany, France. You cannot approach the work too closely without losing a sense of its parameters, a garden, which borders the focus of the work, a judge's robe and wig, apparently hung out to dry on a washing line. Pierre Cavallet was a French judge who as an amateur artist had recorded aspects of his legal career, but this image has been reworked by Young from a snapshot Cavallet made on his retirement from the judiciary. The intimacy of the laundered object, at odds with the grandeur of the ceremony of the law, is the apparent subject matter here. It is an image that beautifully represents, at a sensual level, the quotation I adopted from Brecht earlier: 'it would be easier for a judge's robe and a judge's hat to pass judgment than for a man with no robe and no hat. If you don't treat it with respect, the law just disappears on you.' Here the poignancy of the image has something to do with the imagined way the law has 'disappeared' on Cavallet – the robes hang like a skin emptied of its human contents. But it is the scale of the image and its colour-field sumptuousness that marks this work out as that of Carey Young, who always appears to be engaging her audience with something palpably physical and mobile. Here, the former, vigorous agency of the judge has given way to a 'human void' hanging within the bucolic redundancy of the garden of retirement. Meanwhile, our own encounter with the work is invited, 'called upon', as though Louis Althusser's order of interpellation or 'hailing' was being played out in the gallery.

Consideration (2004-2005) perhaps best exemplifies how Carey Young situates spectators to inscribe their involvement in the staging of the work itself and some kind of faux legal agreement. This is a series of mixed media works that purport to display a sequence of legally enforceable contracts between the artist, Carey Young, who signs many of the legally binding licenses that form part of the work, and the viewer. As with other work, this has been prepared in collaboration with an advisory legal team. Wall mounted text and projected videos combine in these works to draw, performatively one might say after J.L. Austin, the viewer into agreements engaging with questions of individual autonomy and freedom of speech. Throughout the gallery space, in this case again the Paula Cooper Gallery, which must stand as one of the most forensically inscribed gallery spaces in NY, the whole movement of the viewer is one striated and punctuated by protocols with legal implications. This work exposes those subterranean legal dynamics that I referred to earlier as cutting across any aesthetic act as though each, and all, legal determinants in the space have been colour-dyed and made luminous with an infrared light. What one might have thought of as 'neutral' or 'void' space, the modernist white-walled aesthetic of the quintessential Manhattan gallery, is exposed for what it is – a commercially sensitive, legally bound apparatus of contractual complexity and force.

As part of the installation of *Consideration*, 'Declared Void' (a work from 2005) perhaps most directly points us to the 'negative personhood' as identified by Colin Dayan in the dark side of the law. On a corner of the gallery, a black line the width of a goal post has been drawn in a vertical two human figures high, continued around the corner at this height, and dropped down symmetrically on the right angled wall. Another black line has been drawn upon the gallery floor, joining to the line as it meets the floor at its two points and making a lined cube in two dimensions into which any visitor who so wishes can step. It is neither claustrophobic enough to put off visitors nor is it specific enough to unsettle the right to free gallery movement. The text to the side of this marked zone of indeterminacy makes clear what you are doing should you choose to step in, with others or alone. The text over five bold lines reads thus:

BY ENTERING THE ZONE CREATED BY
THIS DRAWING, AND FOR THE PERIOD YOU
REMAIN THERE, YOU DECLARE AND
AGREE THAT THE US CONSTITUTION
WILL NOT APPLY TO YOU.

At one obvious level, this, and many other Carey Young projects that involve 'disclaimers', 'donor cards', 'cautionary statements' and 'artistic licenses', operates as a convoluted joke. Whether it is Carey Young's impulse to make us laugh in the otherwise often po-faced silence of a gallery is not the point. I, and others, do think there is an inherent parodic and comic turn that punctuates almost all of these works, if only at the level of Kafkaesque absurdity. But any such laughter momentarily caught within the paradox of being 'Declared Void' has of course its telling and deeply felt dark side. Especially in a decade marked as this one has been, by the declaration of an almost continuous state of emergency by authorities whose instinct has been to initiate conditions that Karl Schmitt would have described as 'states of exception'.

States of exception

In such states it is not just that the 'rule of law' is suspended, but as importantly that there are new and emerging realms of human activity that are just not subject to the law at all. The precarity of the 'rule of law' is described in the following way by a judge as eminent as Tom Bingham, who in the late 20th century successively held the three highest offices in UK law:

> It might have been supposed that, at the outset of
> the twenty-first century, nothing could be clearer
> than the rejection by civilized nations of torture
> and humiliating and degrading treatment, and

the rejection by civilized courts of the evidential fruits of such conduct. Unhappily ... US officials have, as a deliberate act of policy, rewritten the definition of torture; have inflicted treatment which most of the rest of the world regards as torture and which is now acknowledged by the US Government to be such; and have sought to deny protection against torture or cruel, inhuman and degrading treatment to foreign nationals held abroad, leaving the United States free to do to foreigners abroad what it would not do to Americans at home. (2011, p. 152)

The author of this coruscating critique is hardly a revolutionary. Having been Master of the Rolls, Lord Chief Justice of England and Senior Law Lord of the United Kingdom, three offices one is unlikely to inhabit should one have been of anarchist or left-wing leanings, these words are sobering for their exacting expectations of the law in fraught international circumstances.

But despite the promises on election by President Barack Obama that Camp X Ray at Guantanamo Bay would be closed down during his term of office, the evidence is that incarceration without trial is still prevalent in places where Carey Young's black line has been redrawn with barbed wire, within which the orange jumpsuited detainees are 'declared void' both by their exclusion from the rights of other US citizens under the Constitution, but also, alarmingly, by being surrendered as superfluous by international allies in order to safeguard convivial relations with US interests. Extraordinary rendition is no longer an effusive way of describing a beautiful aria. Rather it has become ubiquitous with the illegal transport of these 'suspects' from one country to another. These extrajudicial acts were initiated by Bill Clinton but subsequently ratcheted up in 2009 by Barack Obama and tolerated or actively supported by successive UK governments as the US Senate Intelligence Committee Report on CIA Torture makes manifest (2014).

It was as early as May 2009 that the Southwark Playhouse in London collaborated with the UK-based charity and activist network Reprieve in staging the *Rendition Monologues*. There have been many verbatim theatrical events that have taken legal narratives as their frame. Most obvious of these are the sequence of 'enquiry' based events pioneered by the Tricycle Theatre in London through the 1990s and early 2000s, including *The Colour of Justice* (concerning the racist murder of Stephen Lawrence), *Deepcut* (exploring suspicious shooting deaths that occurred at a British army barracks) and *The Riots* (in which testimonies of those caught up in the London-wide street protests of 2011 were dramatically rendered both in Kilburn and then, where I saw them, at the Bernie Grant Centre in Tottenham, north London, barely a mile from the well spring of the action). Amongst this plethora of legally related dramatizations the *Rendition Monologues*, the work of the theatre company ice-andfire perhaps serves as the starkest of stagings, concerning the first-hand testimonies of those 'extraneous persons' who became victims of the rendition process, amongst whom the narrative of Binyam Mohamed as a recent resident of Guantanamo Bay stands out.

While this performance and its scripting was on one level the skilled work of Artistic Director Christine Bacon, it is the testimonies themselves that articulated and revealed something of the public secret that had for some time been sustained by a State apparatus, unwilling to admit that Extraordinary Rendition was taking place, nor that UK flight space was being deployed while, arguably, US air bases were being used for refuelling of those human transporters. The 'rendition' (in the theatrical sense) of brutalization of Binyam Mohamed following his 'rendition' (in the extrajudicial sense) to Morocco exposes the effects of a network of State power on the body itself. Any familiarity with the long-running and harrowing case of 'mistaken identity' of Khaled El Masri, a German national whose extradition by the CIA to Afghanistan in 2004 was, in 2012, condemned by 17 judges in the European Court at Strasbourg (with breaches of Convention Articles 3 on torture, 5 on unlawful detention, 8 on private life and 13 on right to an effective remedy), would prepare any listener to the *Rendition Monologues* that this is business as usual in the state of exception. What such prior knowledge cannot prepare audiences for is the precise manner in which the theatrical force of testimony combines affect and effect in a dynamic possibly unique to performance. Open Society Foundations lists 20 pulverizing facts about CIA Extraordinary Rendition and Secret Detention on its web site. The last of these notes that the US Senate Select Intelligence Committee has compiled a 6000-page report on these renditions that remains secret. The imbalance between that 'private' information, and that otherwise veiled knowledge rendered for the public through acts such as *Rendition Monologues*, is a stark measure of the proportionality of power that declares people void, or in the words of Colin Dayan, creates extraneous persons.

There are of course more or less cogent 'reasons' for these abuses, justifications made; the state of exception is not named, but is implied by self-proclaimed 'democracies' at every turn. But there are no excuses in law for this. Here effects of law in such cases should surely pay heed to the widely expressed affects anyone might feel about such things. The Council of Europe states its principles quite explicitly as far back as 2002:

> The temptation of governments and parliaments in countries suffering from terrorist action is to fight fire with fire, setting aside the legal standards that exist in a democratic state. But let us be clear about this ... [the State] may not use indiscriminate measures which would only undermine the fundamental values they seek to protect. (Bingham, pp. 158-159)

My second example of a legally driven process through which a human becomes an extraneous person is one that most overtly complicates Brecht's aspiration that 'the valley go to the waterers that it yield fruit'. So disarmingly coy does that Brechtian adage sound when placed in this new darker context that one is brought up short in the apparent contradictory intensities this book has had to deal with in such brief order. It is hardly that the early 1940s, when Brecht wrote *The Caucasian Chalk Circle*, were years of winsome affection and plenty on the global stage, but rather that the brute politics of these legal and illegal proceedings today strike us with a kind of topical force.

Dale Farm has a bucolic name and a conflicted past. It represents one of the most fought over plots of land in recent British history, a landscape where legal precedents of Traveller protection have become mixed with public perceptions and misconceptions of trespass, squatters' rights, and social exclusion. Covering a six acre site, bordering the busy Southend to London Arterial Road in Essex, since 1982 Dale Farm had served as an 'authorized' Travellers' site with, at the outset, 34 legal pitches for vehicles and families. With the purchase of Dale Farm cottage by Traveller John Sheridan in 2001, the site grew with new residents without planning permission, adding vehicles and chalets to the original community. From 2001 the local council of Basildon was serving enforcement notices on the Travellers, effectively trying to evict them; against these the Travellers, in turn, brought their own legal actions in defence of their rights to inhabit the land. The Council began to describe the terrain as part of the sanctified 'Green Belt' despite the fact that for years it had been concreted over with hard standing to allow for vehicle use. Successive enquiries ruled that the site was illegal in law. A temporary stay against eviction was awarded by the then Labour government while up to 400 people who faced homelessness with eviction might find a 'suitable alternative site'. Between 2007 and 2010 a succession of judicial rulings was followed by appeals; these culminated in the High Court in 2008 in the Travellers winning the right to stay, only to see that ruling reversed on appeal in 2010. In the midst of this process, Essex Council's own Racial Equality Unit part-funded a community centre on the site for the Travellers that was, in keeping with everything else there, built without planning permission.

In September 2011, further eviction proceedings began with an orchestrated plan by Basildon Council to clear the land. Camp Constant, built on the site during this period, was joined by activists from across Europe in solidarity with the residents and to resist the eviction. At this point, hearings were still taking place in the Appeal Court on the Strand, where I heard court evidence from Mary Sheridan and other residents given to Mr Justice Edwards-Stuart, who, apparently sympathetic to their articulate and impassioned arguments, issued an injunction against the evictions on the grounds that they may go further than the law permitted through the enforcement notices that had been awarded to the Council. But by October, with reassurances regarding the maintenance of power supplies to the residents, the same judge was agreeing that 49 of the 54 plots could be cleared, while walls and fences would have to remain as they were. This concern for the maintenance of the dividing partitions of the space, as distinct to the occupants of the space itself, struck me as an onlooker as a peculiar rider to what seemed like a comprehensive and draconian action against 400 Travellers of whom 100 were children mostly attending a local school. But I had underestimated the historic and critical place such boundaries, internal or otherwise, play within English law with its continuous history of disputation over land and rights, which are in the end always disagreements about boundaries and borders.

Further delays occurred while three separate judicial reviews were considered, only for Mr Justice Ouseley, one of the UK's most experienced judges, to rule in October against the appeals and the Travellers. Previously Ouseley had rejected appeals by suspected international terrorists against indefinite detention, a decision that was overturned in 2004 when the House of Lords ruled that it violated the Human Rights Act. Yet another judge, with the capacious name, Lord Justice Jeremy Mirth Sullivan, advised the Travellers that they could not in law change this final decision, and the eviction was restarted by Basildon Council, led by the 'villain' of the peace, Council Leader Tony Ball, whose centrality to the eviction process had brought him a notoriety and public profile he did not appear to have resisted. Meanwhile, fortification by the activists and residents had secured the site from the officials. More than 100 riot police entered the site through the rear fenced area with 200 bailiffs following them in clearing the land of the 'unlawful' buildings that in some cases had stood there for 40 years. Later that day residents left the site, some simply setting up pitches on the adjoining roads between the site and the A127 road.

There is no need to evoke common clichés of 'Irishness', 'Gypsy Lore' or 'Romany Tradition' to realize the dehumanizing effects of this durational legal process for those de-personed by it. Indeed Katharine Quarmby more accurately reflects the complexity of the term Traveller, and through naming conjures their complex presence, when she describes the residents of Dale Farm as: 'English and Scotch Romanies, Welsh Kale Romanies, Irish Travellers, British Showpeople and (New) Travellers ... the Horsedrawns and the Boaters' (2013, p. ix). I recall at the Appeal Court hearing that some supportive activists in the public gallery were circulating evidence of precedent in English Law under which they believed the residents' appeal might be granted. The source of that precedent for Travellers? Precisely laws pertaining to the protection of 'Showpeople', including, but not only, circus travellers who would have been presumed to be peripatetic in their inhabitation of this green and septic isle.

While 'Travelling Showpeople' in the UK do not 'enjoy' all the, albeit circumscribed, rights of 'Gypsies' in UK Law, they can appeal to a range of nationally and internationally recognized measures, including the Town and Country Planning Act of 1990, the Housing Act of 2004 and of course the Human Rights Act of 1988, for definition and protection in law. Ironically at one stage in the proceedings at the High Court, it looked possible that a group of residents simply seeking to be allowed to continue to live as they had been doing, in a small corner of concreted England, would have to be redefined as 'Showpeople' for the purposes of their better protection from eviction and persecution. Mary Sheridan and her neighbours present in that courtroom had no need of such redefinition in law, standing for their livelihoods and their lives with more clarity and confidence than some of the 'professionals' present could muster on their behalf.

While the Sheridans and their neighbours seemed ill-served by the law in the Royal Courts of Justice, there was someone watching proceedings who found a remarkable way to represent, in visual and performance form, what the law seemed destined to conceal. Lynne McCarthy describes her collaboration with three Traveller women and artists Kelly Green and Hannah Sharkey, *Soil Depositions*, as an 'art activist project' that cherished some soil from the Dale Farm site, donated by the three women, and relocated it to other symbolically significant sites in the UK and beyond, from Parliament Square London to the Olympic site in Brazil. The action took place on United Nations International Migrants Day, the 18th December, just two months after the eviction had taken place. These acts drew upon Lauren Berlant's idea of 'impasse', in McCarthy's terms, 'an affective descriptor of the post-eviction situation', and symbolically through the repositioning of the donated soil in mundane public situations explored 'the unresolved nature of Traveller claims to property'. Here, through a performative process of restaging the soil, McCarthy and her collaborators seek to make visible 'property rights' for what they are, a structural apparatus that 'condition the agency of the user'. Furthermore the limpid quality of the performative action is backed up, in this case, by a forensically astute analysis combining in-depth legal precedents through which McCarthy explores misunderstandings between 'sedentarist' and 'nomadic' property values, definitions of soil as a commodity form, and the impasse of those caught between the legal imperative to travel, ruptured from their human rights to reside (McCarthy, 2015). The proximity of the words reside and desire as anagrams in affective association should not be missed here.

Colin Dayan would recognize the primary place the affective has been afforded within McCarthy's pungent critique of the ineffectiveness of the law. She would equally eschew all romance in her caustic view of these processes, but interestingly for all that, not ignore the palpable spectral quality of the consequences of such actions of oppression. She rather puts it like this: 'The ghosts of the ancestors always return. What is abused and damaged rises up to haunt. Persons judged outside the law's protection and marked as enemies of the community resort to an alternative understanding of the law. Degraded and socially excluded, they interpret legal precepts and proscriptions for themselves and reconvene the rules: not the opposite of law but its haunting' (2011, p. 252).

The actor and campaigner Corin Redgrave, perhaps (unfortunately) better known for featuring in the film *Four Weddings and a Funeral* (1994) than his lifelong campaigning against injustices, knew this very well. In an attempt to generate support amongst the local councillors for the residents of Dale Farm in 2005 he had made a speech at the Towngate Theatre Basildon, as part of a public meeting to which 300 people had come, immediately after which he suffered a 'massive' heart attack from which he never fully recovered. He had called the Travellers 'the most deprived community in the country' on that occasion. According to his sister Vanessa, who was on another stage in the US playing Hecuba at the time (a mother who with 19 children knew a thing or two about sacrifice), Corin would have died had a Traveller not administered mouth-to-mouth resuscitation on him. There is an easy way in which the diarists in the media might parody and pillory such seriousness of conviction amongst those who are denied any rights to seriousness by nature of their professional vocation, theatre. It did not need Michael Fried in the 1960s to monster 'theatricality' and its falsities to alert us to this cliché, an anti-theatrical prejudice that has been alive and well since Plato. But it would be peculiar given the continuous relations between theatre and law I have sketched out in this book should actors not consider it wholly in keeping with their identity to assume responsibility for the expression of legal rights and wrongs. Actors as I suggested at the outset might always have considered themselves advocates first.

Six years after Corin Redgrave's collapse, and a year after his death, in 2011 at the moment of the Dale Farm evictions, this 'speech' was itself resuscitated by his widow Kika Markham on the stage of Augusto Boal's *Théâtre de L'Opprimé* in Paris. In an irony of casting that wholly bears out the complicating of cause and effect in this book, Markham is perhaps herself better known as having featured in Lynda la Plante's landmark television series, *Trial and Retribution* (2000), playing a judge, to Corin Redgrave's barrister.

To note that their only other screen appearance together was as lovers suspected of murdering a government advisor in the BBC series *Waking the Dead* is to emphasize some already well-explored interrelations between theatre and law, legalism and larceny. On that occasion Markham shared the stage, in support of the Dale Farm residents, with the actress Anna Cartaret, perhaps better known as police inspector Kate Longton in 1980s 'cop' drama, *Juliet Bravo*. One might have been forgiven, on looking at the cast list on that evening at the *Théâtre de L'Opprimé*, for thinking that these performers were peculiarly well-suited to the occasion and they had perhaps, as I had once felt as Azdak, known that the relations between theatre and law were always omnipresent, sometimes oppressive and sometimes opportunities for the mobilization of serious *effects* as well as the site for the pleasure and pain of affects. And the abiding spirit of that very theatre, the founder of the Theatre of the Oppressed movement, Augusto Boal, might well have looked on from his Forum Theatre in the clouds, where problems with divine law have been detaining him, and remembered that when on this earth, as city councillor in Rio de Janeiro, his own 'legislative theatre' had created a slate of wholly new, abiding laws that in their humour and humanity might have well served these newly minted 'extraneous persons' in their quest to find themselves in this state of exception.

further reading

Given their centrality to the writing of this book, 'Before the Law' and 'In the Penal Colony' by Kafka might be short stories to return to. Brecht's *The Caucasian Chalk Circle* always rewards reading, seeing and playing, as would Elevator Repair Service's *Arguendo*. Canonical dramatic texts such as Aristophanes' *Wasps*, Shakespeare's *The Merchant of Venice*, and Miller's *The Crucible* should not be ignored for their representations of law. Theoretically, two compendia stand out that in their breadth and depth would supplement with practised examples almost every aspect of this book: Leiboff and Nield's 'Law's Theatrical Presence', edited for *Law Text Culture* (2010), includes telling work by the editors themselves alongside Bachmann, Schmidt and White, amongst many others; Wagner and Sherwin's edited collection *Law, Culture and Visual Studies* (2014) includes an excellent essay on the semiotics of the criminal trial by Brion amidst much else of interest. Helen

Freshwater's *Theatre Censorship in Britain* and Nicholas Harrison's *Circles of Censorship* are comprehensive in their discussions of censorship in the UK and France. I have given scant attention to Boal, whose *Legislative Theatre* is a suggestive work, and have rather characteristically avoided Shakespeare, knowing that work by Watt and Raffield, and Ward is exemplary, while Mukherji offers fine detail on representations of law in the Early Modern. The work of the artist/activist group Platform over a quarter of a century has insisted on the legal dimension of resistance to oppression at every turn, and their website rewards close attention. Dayan's exploration of the unmaking of persons through law is salutary, indeed, essential reading, as will be the work of McCarthy on the plight of the Dale Farm Travellers. Halliday's magisterial work, *Habeas Corpus*, demonstrates the sinuous relations between law and its performance that this book sought to mimic in small measure.

Bibliography

Agamben, Giorgio. *The Sacrament of Language*. Trans. Adam Kotsko. Cambridge: Polity, 2011.

———. *State of Exception*. Trans. Kevin Attell. Chicago: University of Chicago Press, 2005.

Arendt, Hannah. *The Origins of Totalitarianism*. London: Allen and Unwin, 1967.

Aristophanes. 'Wasps', in *Frogs and Other Plays*. Trans. David Barrett. London: Penguin, 1964, 9–70.

Auslander, Phillip. *Liveness*. London: Routledge, 1999.

Austin, John. *The Province of Jurisprudence Determined*. London, 1832.

Austin, J.L. *How to Do Things with Words*. Oxford: Oxford UP, 1962.

Baker, J.H. *An Introduction to English Legal History*. Oxford: Oxford UP, 2002.

Benjamin, Walter. 'Critique of Violence', in *Selected Writings Volume 1. 1913-1926*. Ed. and Trans. Marcus Bullock and Michael W. Jennings. Cambridge: Harvard UP, 2002, 236–252.

Bergman, Paul and Asimow, Michael. *Reel Justice: The Courtroom Goes to the Movies*. Kansas: Andrews and McMeel, 1996.

Bharucha, Rustom. *Terror and Performance*. Abingdon: Routledge, 2014.

Bingham, Tom. *The Rule of Law*. London: Penguin, 2011.

Boal, Augusto. *Legislative Theatre: Using Performance to Make Politics*. London: Routledge, 1998.

Bond, Edward. *Saved*. London: Methuen, 1966.

Bowcott, Owen. 'UK among Worst in Europe for Employing Female Judges' in *The Guardian*, Thursday 20th September 2012. http://www.theguardian.com/law/2012/sep/20/uk-female-judges-ratio-europe

Bravin, Jess. *The Terror Courts: Rough Justice at Guantanamo Bay*. New Haven: Yale UP, 2013.

Brecht, Bertolt. *The Caucasian Chalk Circle*. Ed. and Trans. Eric Bentley. London: Penguin, 1975.

Brenton, Howard. 'The Romans in Britain', in *Brenton: Plays 2*. London: Methuen, 1989.

Burgess, John and Marowitz, Charles. 'The Chicago Conspiracy', in *Open Space Plays*. Ed. Charles Marowitz. London: Penguin, 1974.

Butler, Judith. *Excitable Speech*. New York: Routledge, 1997.

———. *Gender Trouble*. London: Routledge, 1990.

Cassin, Barbara. Ed. *Dictionary of Untranslatables*. Princeton: Princeton UP, 2014.

Chandler, Charlotte. *Not the Girl Next Door*. New York: Simon & Schuster; 2008.

Charles, Casey. *Critical Queer Studies: Law, Film and Fiction in Contemporary American Culture*. Farnham: Ashgate, 2012.

Croce, Mariano and Salvatore, Andrea. *The Legal Theory of Carl Schmitt*. Abingdon: Routledge, 2013.

Dayan, Colin. *The Law Is a White Dog: How Legal Rituals Make and Unmake Persons*. Princeton: Princeton UP, 2011.

Derrida, Jacques. *The Death Penalty*. Ed. Geoffrey Bennington et al. Trans. Peggy Kamuf. Chicago: University of Chicago Press, 2014.

Dickens, Charles. *Bleak House*. London: Penguin, 2003.

Doughty, Louise. 'The 10 Best Courtroom Dramas' in *The Guardian*, Friday 14th February 2014. http://www.theguardian.com/culture/gallery/2014/feb/14/the-10-best-courtroom-dramas

Drakopoulou, Maria. Ed. *Feminist Encounters with Legal Philosophy*. Abingdon: Routledge, 2013.

Dresch, Paul and Skoda, Hannah. Eds. *Legalism: Anthropology and History*. Oxford: Oxford UP, 2012.

Dworkin, Ronald. *Law's Empire*. Cambridge: Belknap, 1986.

Eliot, George. *Middlemarch*. Ware: Wordsworth, 1994.

Foucault, Michel. *Discipline and Punish*. Trans. Alan Sheridan. New York: Knopf, 2012.

Freshwater, Helen. *Theatre Censorship in Britain: Silencing, Censure and Suppression*. Houndmills: Palgrave, 2009.

Galli, Carlo. *Political Spaces and Global War*. Ed. Adam Sitze. Trans. Elizabeth Fay. Minneapolis: University of Minnesota Press, 2010.

Geertz, Clifford. 'Local Knowledge: Fact and Law in Comparative Perspective', in *Local Knowledge*. Ed. Clifford Geertz. New York: Basic Books, 1983.

Halliday, Paul. *Habeas Corpus: From England to Empire*. Cambridge: Harvard UP, 2010.

Hammond, Will and Steward, Dan. Eds. *Verbatim, Verbatim: Contemporary Documentary Theatre*. London: Oberon, 2007.

Hare, David. *Murmuring Judges*. London: Faber, 1993.

Harrison, Nicholas. *Circles of Censorship: Censorship and its Metaphors in French History, Literature and Theory*. Oxford: Oxford UP, 1995.

Heller-Roazen, Daniel. *The Enemy of All: Piracy and the Law of Nations*. New York: Zone Books, 2009.

Hobbes, Thomas. *A Dialogue Between a Philosopher and a Student of the Common Laws of England*. Ed. Joseph Cropsey. Chicago: Chicago UP, 1971.

Kafka, Franz. *The Complete Novels*. Trans. Willa and Edwin Muir. London: Vintage, 1992.

———. 'Before the Law', and 'In the Penal Colony', in *The Complete Short Stories*. Ed. Nahum N. Glazer. London: Vintage Books, 2005.

Kearns, Paul. *Freedom of Artistic Expression: Essays on Culture and Legal Censure*. Oxford: Hart Publishing, 2013.

Laclau, Ernesto. *The Rhetorical Foundations of Society*. London: Verso, 2014.

Lee, Harper. *To Kill a Mockingbird*. London: Vintage, 2004.

Leiboff, Marett and Nield, Sophie. Eds. 'Law's Theatrical Presence' (special issue) *Law Text Culture*, Vol. 14, No. 1, 2010.

Luhmann, Niklas. *Law as a Social System*. Ed. Fatimer Kastner et al. Trans. Klaus A. Ziegart. Oxford: Oxford UP, 2004.

McCarthy, Lynne. 'Aesthetics at the Impasse: The Unresolved Property at Dale Farm' *Research in Drama Education*, Vol. 20, No. 1, 74–86, 2015.

McDonagh, Luke. 'Plays, Performance and Power Struggles – Examining Copyright's "Integrity" in the Field of Theatre' *The Modern Law Review*, Vol. 77, No. 4, 533–562, 2014.

Miller, Arthur. *The Crucible*. London: Penguin, 2000.

Mitropoulos, Angela. *Contract and Contagion: From Biopolitics to Oikonomia*. Wivenhoe: Minor Compositions, 2012.

Mukherji, S. *Law and Representation in Early Modern Drama*. Cambridge: Cambridge UP, 2006.

Nichols, Joshua. *The End(s) of Community: History, Sovereignty and the Question of Law*. Waterloo: Wilfred Laurier UP, 2013.

Norton-Taylor, Richard. *The Colour of Justice*. London: Oberon, 1999.

———. *Bloody Sunday: Scenes from the Saville Enquiry*. London: Oberon, 2005.

O'Brien, Aidan C. 'Nothing but the Truth' in *The Guardian*, Tuesday 22nd May, 2012.

Ophir, Adi. *The Order of Evils: Toward an Ontology of Morals*. Trans. Rela Mazali and Havi Carel. New York: Zone, 2005.

Pastoureau, Michel. *The Devil's Cloth: A History of Stripes and Striped Fabric*. Columbia: Columbia UP, 1991.

Pirie, Fernanda. *The Anthropology of Law*. Oxford: Oxford UP, 2013.

Plato. *The Laws*. Trans. Trevor J. Saunders. London: Penguin, 2004.

Quarmby, Katharine. *No Place to Call Home*. London: Oneworld, 2013.

Rae, Paul. *Theatre & Human Rights*. (With a Foreword by Rabih Mroue.) Houndmills: Palgrave, 2009.

Raffield, Paul. *Images and Culture of Law in Early Modern England*. Cambridge: Cambridge UP, 2007.

Ralph, Phillip. *Deep Cut*. London: Oberon, 2009.

Read, Alan. 'Fifth Approach: Psychological and Legal', in *Theatre in the Expanded Field: Seven Approaches to Performance*. London: Bloomsbury, 2013, 113–148.

———. 'Combustion', in *Theatre & Everyday Life: An Ethics of Performance*. London: Routledge, 1993, 228–236.

———. *Theatre, Intimacy & Engagement. The Last Human Venue*. Houndmills: Palgrave, 2008.

Robson, Ruthann. 'Traditional Court Dress', in *Dressing Constitutionally: Hierarchy, Sexuality and Democracy from our Hairstyles to our Shoes*. Cambridge: Cambridge UP, 2013, 97–102.

Rose, Gillian. *The Broken Middle*. Oxford: Blackwell, 1992.

Schechner, Richard. *Essays on Performance Theory, 1970-1976*. New York: Drama Publishers, 1976.

Searle, John. *Speech Acts: An Essay in the Philosophy of Language*. Cambridge: Cambridge UP, 1969.

Sedley, Stephen. *Ashes and Sparks: Essays on Law and Justice*. Cambridge: Cambridge UP, 2011.

Sen, Amartya. *The Idea of Justice*. London: Penguin, 2009.

Shakespeare, William. *Measure for Measure*. Ed. J.W. Lever. The Arden Shakespeare. London: Methuen, 1977.

———. *The Merchant of Venice*. Ed. John Drakakis. London: Bloomsbury, 2010.

Sitze, Adam. 'Capital Punishment as a Problem for the Philosophy of Law' *The New Centennial Review*, Vol. 9, No. 2, 221–270, 2009.

Slovo, Gillian. *The Riots*. London: Oberon, 2011.

Steinberg, Erwin, R. 'The Judgment in Kafka's "In The Penal Colony"' *Journal of Modern Literature*, Vol. 5, No. 3, p. 492, Indiana University Press, 1976.

Supiot, Alain. *Homo Juridicus: On the Anthropological Function of the Law*. Trans. Saskia Brown. London: Verso, 2007.

de Sutter, Laurent. *Althusser and Law*. Abingdon: Routledge, 2013.

Thirlwall, Justice. *Judgment*. Between the Queen, on the application of Mr Steven Earl and Winchester City Council. Neutral Citation Number: [2014] EWHC 195 (admin). Royal Courts of Justice, London, 5th February 2014.

Turner, Victor. *From Ritual to Theatre: The Human Seriousness of Play*. New York: Performing Arts Journal Publications, 1982.

Wagner, Anne and Sherwin, Richard K. Eds. *Law, Culture and Visual Studies*. London: Springer, 2014, especially: 'The Criminal Trial as Theater: The Semiotic Power of the Image', Denis J. Brion, 329–359.

Ward, I. *Shakespeare and the Legal Imagination*. Cambridge: Cambridge UP, 1999.

Watt, G. and Raffield, P. *Shakespeare and the Law*. Oxford: Hart, 2008.

Websites

Carey Young. http://www.careyyoung.com/main.php (Accessed 26/09/2014)

Elevator Repair Service. https://www.elevator.org/shows/arguendo/ (Accessed 26/09/2014)

Performance Foundation, Out Law. http://www.kcl.ac.uk/artshums/depts/english/about/performance/foundation.aspx (Accessed 26/09/2014)

Platform. http://platformlondon.org (Accessed 26/09/2014)

Theatres Act 1968. http://www.legislation.gov.uk/ukpga/1968/54 (Accessed 26/09/2014)

Tricycle Theatre. http://www.tricycle.co.uk/home/about-the-tricycle-pages/about-us-tab-menu/archive/archived-theatre-production/ (Accessed 26/09/2014)

index

acknowledgements

I am indebted to Chris Johnston QC, and Amy Street, curator and barrister, Serjeants' Inn Chambers, and Ben Bowling, Professor of Criminology and Criminal Justice at King's College London, with whom these ideas have been shared as part of our work, through the Performance Foundation, on Out Law. Jen Harvie edited this book with forensic care and, together with Dan Rebellato, brought it about. An anonymous reader invited welcome improvements. Barbara Villez convened the exceptional Performing the Law conference in collaboration with Paris 8 and Birkbeck College at the French Institute in London in 2014, the proceedings of which shaped the opening chapter of this book, especially the work of: Daniel Monk, Carey Young, Guy Spielmann, Leslie J. Moran, Gary Watt, and John Collins. Aoife Monks was persuasive with her responses there. Cristina Marinho of Porto University curated the Law and Performance symposium in 2014 and I benefited from the work of Isabelle Ost, Jose Carlos Andrade, Christian Biet and Maria Aristodemou. Michael Bachmann alerted me to critical resources I had overlooked. Lynne McCarthy shared her doctoral research on Dale Farm with great generosity. Geoff Winslow cast me in the role of Azdak in *The Caucasian Chalk Circle* in 1973, an act of faith with lasting repercussions, while Professor John Barton of Merton College Oxford had the foresight to suggest playing such a role did not necessarily equip me for a life in law, and that theatre might be an alternative worth considering. Successive years of students from Boston University (since 1991), Roehampton University (since 1997) and King's College London (since 2006) have accompanied me to the Royal Courts of Justice and tolerated my fascination with the Daily Cause List. This book is dedicated to them, and to other students, whether within or, as in the case of Mr Earl, without the law.

contents

For Students
Legal & Illegal